CAMBRIDGE
UNIVERSITY PRESS

Biology

for Cambridge International AS & A Level

EXAM PREPARATION AND PRACTICE

Katie Estruch & Rachel Wong

Contents

A Level

There are extra digital questions for this title found online at Cambridge GO.
For more information on how to access and use your digital resource, please see inside the front cover.

> How to use this series

This suite of resources supports students and teachers following the Cambridge International AS & A Level Biology syllabus (9700). All of the components in the series are designed to work together and help students develop the necessary knowledge and skills for this subject. With clear language and style, they are designed for international students.

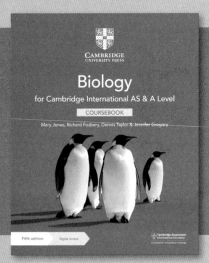

The coursebook provides comprehensive support for the full Cambridge International Biology syllabus (9700). It includes exercises that develop problem-solving skills, practical activities to help students develop investigative skills, and real world examples of scientific principles. With clear language and style, the coursebook is designed for international learners.

The teacher's resource supports and enhances the projects, questions and practical activities in the coursebook. This resource includes detailed lesson ideas, as well as answers and exemplar data for all questions and activities in the coursebook and workbook. The practical teacher's guide, included with this resource, provides support for the practical activities and experiments in the practical workbook.

The workbook contains over 100 extra activities that help students build on what they have learned in the coursebook. Students can practise their experimentation, analysis and evaluation skills through exercises testing problem solving and data handling, while activities also support students' planning and investigative skills.

Hands-on investigations provide opportunities to develop key scientific skills, including planning investigations, identifying equipment, creating hypotheses, recording results, and analysing and evaluating data.

The Exam Preparation and Practice resource provides dedicated support for learners in preparing for their final assessments. Hundreds of questions in the book and accompanying digital resource will help learners to check that they understand, and can recall, syllabus concepts. To help learners to show what they know in an exam context, a checklist of exam skills with corresponding questions, and past paper question practice, is also included. Self-assessment and reflection features support learners to identify any areas that need further practice. This resource should be used alongside the coursebook, throughout the course of study, so learners can most effectively increase their confidence and readiness for their exams.

> How to use this book

This book will help you to check that you **know** the content of the syllabus and practise how to **show** this understanding in an exam. It will also help you be cognitively prepared and in the **flow**, ready for your exam. Research has shown that it is important that you do all three of these things, so we have designed the Know, Show, Flow approach to help you prepare effectively for exams.

| Know | You will need to consolidate and then recall a lot of syllabus content. |

| Show | You should demonstrate your knowledge in the context of a Cambridge exam. |

| Flow | You should be cognitively engaged and ready to learn. This means reducing test anxiety. |

Exam skills checklist

Category	Exam skill
Understanding the question	Recognise different question types
	Understand command words
	Mark scheme awareness
Providing an appropriate response	Understand connections between concepts
	Keep to time
	Know what a good answer looks like
Developing supportive behaviours	Reflect on progress
	Manage test anxiety

This **Exam skills checklist** helps you to develop the awareness, behaviours and habits that will support you when revising and preparing for your exams. For more exam skills advice, including understanding command words and managing your time effectively, please go to the **Exam skills chapter**.

Know

The full syllabus content of your AS & A Level Biology course is covered in your Cambridge coursebook. This book will provide you with different types of questions to support you as you prepare for your exams. You will answer **Knowledge recall questions** that are designed to make sure you understand a topic, and **Recall and connect questions** to help you recall past learning and connect different concepts.

KNOWLEDGE FOCUS

Knowledge focus boxes summarise the topics that you will answer questions on in each chapter of this book. You can refer back to your Cambridge coursebook to remind yourself of the full detail of the syllabus content.

Knowledge recall questions

Testing yourself is a good way to check that your understanding is secure. These questions will help you to recall the core knowledge you have acquired during your course, and highlight any areas where you may need more practice. They are indicated with a blue bar with a gap, at the side of the page. We recommend that you answer the Knowledge recall questions just after you have covered the relevant topic in class, and then return to them at a later point to check you have properly understood the content.

≪ RECALL AND CONNECT ≪

To consolidate your learning, you need to test your memory frequently. These questions will test that you remember what you learned in previous chapters, in addition to what you are practising in the current chapter.

UNDERSTAND THESE TERMS

These list the important vocabulary that you should understand for each chapter. Definitions are provided in the glossary of your Cambridge coursebook.

Show

Exam questions test specific knowledge, skills and understanding. You need to be prepared so that you have the best opportunity to show what you know in the time you have during the exam. In addition to practising recall of the syllabus content, it is important to build your exam skills throughout the year.

EXAM SKILLS FOCUS

This feature outlines the exam skills you will practise in each chapter, alongside the Knowledge focus. They are drawn from the core set of eight exam skills, listed in the Exam skills checklist. You will practise specific exam skills, such as understanding command words, within each chapter. More general exam skills, such as managing text anxiety, are covered in the Exam skills chapter.

Exam skills questions

These questions will help you to develop your exam skills and demonstrate your understanding. To help you become familiar with exam-style questioning, many of these questions follow the style and use the language of real exam questions, and have allocated marks. They are indicated with a solid red bar at the side of the page.

Looking at sample answers to past paper questions helps you to understand what to aim for.

The **Exam practice** sections in this resource contain example student responses and examiner-style commentary showing how the answer could be improved (both written by the authors).

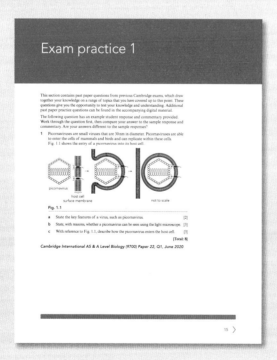

Flow

Preparing for exams can be stressful. One of the approaches recommended by educational psychologists to help with this stress is to improve behaviours around exam preparation. This involves testing yourself in manageable chunks, accompanied by self-evaluation. You should avoid cramming and build in more preparation time. This book is structured to help you do this.

Increasing your ability to recognise the signs of exam-related stress and working through some techniques for how to cope with it will help to make your exam preparation manageable.

REFLECTION

This feature asks you to think about the approach that you take to your exam preparation, and how you might improve this in the future. Reflecting on how you plan, monitor and evaluate your revision and preparation will help you to do your best in your exams.

SELF-ASSESSMENT CHECKLIST

These checklists return to the Learning intentions from your coursebook, as well as the Exam skills focus boxes from each chapter. Checking in on how confident you feel in each of these areas will help you to focus your exam preparation. The 'Show it' prompts will allow you to test your rating. You should revisit any areas that you rate 'Needs more work' or 'Almost there'.

Now I can:	Show it	Needs more work	Almost there	Confident to move on

Increasing your ability to recognise the signs of exam-related stress and working through some techniques for how to cope with it will help to make your exam preparation manageable. The **Exam skills chapter** will support you with this.

Digital support

Extra self-assessment questions for all chapters can be found online at Cambridge GO. For more information on how to access and use your digital resource, please see inside the front cover.

You will find **Answers** for all of the questions in the book on the 'supporting resources' area of the Cambridge GO platform.

Multiple choice questions

These ask you to select the correct answer to a question from four options. These are auto-marked and feedback is provided.

Flip card questions

These present a question on one screen, and suggested answers on the reverse.

Syllabus assessment objectives for AS & A Level Biology

You should be familiar with the Assessment Objectives from the syllabus, as the examiner will be looking for evidence of these requirements in your responses and allocating marks accordingly.

The assessment objectives for this syllabus are:

Assessment objective	AS Level weighting	A Level weighting
AO1: Knowledge and Understanding	30%	25%
AO2: Application	30%	25%
AO3: Analysis	20%	25%
AO4: Evaluation	20%	25%

Exam skills

by Lucy Parsons

What's the point of this book?

Most students make one really basic mistake when they're preparing for exams. What is it? It's focusing far too much on learning 'stuff' – that's facts, figures, ideas, information – and not nearly enough time practising exam skills.

The students who work really, really hard but are disappointed with their results are nearly always students who focus on memorising stuff. They think to themselves, 'I'll do practice papers once I've revised everything.' The trouble is, they start doing practice papers too late to really develop and improve how they communicate what they know.

What could they do differently?

When your final exam script is assessed, it should contain specific language, information and thinking skills in your answers. If you read a question in an exam and you have no idea what you need to do to give a good answer, the likelihood is that your answer won't be as brilliant as it could be. That means your grade won't reflect the hard work you've put into revising for the exam.

There are different types of questions used in exams to assess different skills. You need to know how to recognise these question types and understand what you need to show in your answers.

So, how do you understand what to do in each question type?

That's what this book is all about. But first a little background.

Meet Benjamin Bloom

The psychologist Benjamin Bloom developed a way of classifying and valuing different skills we use when we learn, such as analysis and recalling information. We call these thinking skills. It's known as Bloom's Taxonomy and it's what most exam questions are based around.

If you understand Bloom's Taxonomy, you can understand what any type of question requires you to do. So, what does it look like?

Bloom's Taxonomy of thinking skills

Increasing difficulty →

- Evaluation — **Passing judgement** on something
- Synthesis — **Putting together knowledge,** understanding, application and analysis **to create something new**
- Analysis — **Taking apart** information or data in order to **discover relationships**, motives, causes, patterns and connections
- Application — **Using knowledge** and understanding in **new and different circumstances**
- Understanding — **Distinguishing between two similar ideas** or things by using knowledge to **recognise the difference**
- Knowledge — **Recalling, memorising and knowing**

The key things to take away from this diagram are:

- Knowledge and understanding are known as lower-level thinking skills. They are less difficult than the other thinking skills. Exam questions that just test you on what you know are usually worth the lowest number of marks.

- All the other thinking skills are worth higher numbers of marks in exam questions. These questions need you to have some foundational knowledge and understanding but are far more about how you think than what you know. They involve:

  - Taking what you know and using it in unfamiliar situations (application).

  - Going deeper into information to discover relationships, motives, causes, patterns and connections (analysis).

  - Using what you know and think to create something new – whether that's an essay, long-answer exam question, a solution to a maths problem, or a piece of art (synthesis).

  - Assessing the value of something, e.g. the reliability of the results of a scientific experiment (evaluation).

In this introductory chapter, you'll be shown how to develop the skills that enable you to communicate what you know and how you think. This will help you achieve to the best of your abilities. In the rest of the book, you'll have a chance to practise these exam skills by understanding how questions work and understanding what you need to show in your answers.

Every time you pick up this book and do a few questions, you're getting closer to achieving your dream results. So, let's get started!

Exam preparation and revision skills

What is revision?

If you think about it, the word 'revision' has two parts to it:

• re – which means 'again'

• vision – which is about seeing.

So, revision is literally about 'seeing again'. This means you're looking at something that you've already learned.

Typically, a teacher will teach you something in class. You may then do some questions on it, write about it in some way, or even do a presentation. You might then have an end-of-topic test sometime later. To prepare for this test, you need to 'look again' or revise what you were originally taught.

Step 1: Making knowledge stick

Every time you come back to something you've learned or revised you're improving your understanding and memory of that particular piece of knowledge. This is called **spaced retrieval**. This is how human memory works. If you don't use a piece of knowledge by recalling it, you lose it.

Everything we learn has to be physically stored in our brains by creating neural connections – joining brain cells together. The more often we 'retrieve' or recall a particular piece of knowledge, the stronger the neural connection gets. It's like lifting weights – the more often you lift, the stronger you get.

However, if you don't use a piece of knowledge for a long time, your brain wants to recycle the brain cells and use them for another purpose. The neural connections get weaker until they finally break, and the memory has gone. This is why it's really important to return often to things that you've learned in the past.

Great ways of doing this in your revision include:

• Testing yourself using flip cards – use the ones available in the digital resources for this book.

• Testing yourself (or getting someone else to test you) using questions you've created about the topic.

• Checking your recall of previous topics by answering the Recall and connect questions in this book.

• Blurting – writing everything you can remember about a topic on a piece of paper in one colour. Then, checking what you missed out and filling it in with another colour. You can do this over and over again until you feel confident that you remember everything.

• Answering practice questions – use the ones in this book.

• Getting a good night's sleep to help consolidate your learning.

> **The importance of sleep and creating long-term memory**
>
> When you go to sleep at night, your brain goes through an important process of taking information from your short-term memory and storing it in your long-term memory.
>
> This means that getting a good night's sleep is a very important part of revision. If you don't get enough good quality sleep, you'll actually be making your revision much, much harder.

Step 2: Developing your exam skills

We've already talked about the importance of exam skills, and how many students neglect them because they're worried about covering all the knowledge.

What actually works best is developing your exam skills at the same time as learning the knowledge.

What does this look like in your studies?

- Learning something at school and your teacher setting you questions from this book or from past papers. This tests your recall as well as developing your exam skills.

- Choosing a topic to revise, learning the content and then choosing some questions from this book to test yourself at the same time as developing your exam skills.

The reason why practising your exam skills is so important is that it helps you to get good at communicating what you know and what you think. The more often you do that, the more fluent you'll become in showing what you know in your answers.

Step 3: Getting feedback

The final step is to get feedback on your work.

If you're testing yourself, the feedback is what you got wrong or what you forgot. This means you then need to go back to those things to remind yourself or improve your understanding. Then, you can test yourself again and get more feedback. You can also congratulate yourself for the things you got right – it's important to celebrate any success, big or small.

If you're doing past paper questions or the practice questions in this book, you will need to mark your work. Marking your work is one of the most important things you can do to improve. It's possible to make significant improvements in your marks in a very short space of time when you start marking your work.

Why is marking your own work so powerful? It's because it teaches you to identify the strengths and weaknesses of your own work. When you look at the mark scheme and see how it's structured, you will understand what is needed in your answers to get the results you want.

This doesn't just apply to the knowledge you demonstrate in your answers. It also applies to the language you use and whether it's appropriately subject-specific, the structure of your answer, how you present it on the page and many other factors. Understanding, practising and improving on these things are transformative for your results.

The most important thing about revision

The most important way to make your revision successful is to make it active.

Sometimes, students say they're revising when they sit staring at their textbook or notes for hours at a time. However, this is a really ineffective way to revise because it's passive. In order to make knowledge and skills stick, you need to be doing something like the suggestions in the following diagram. That's why testing yourself and pushing yourself to answer questions that test higher-level thinking skills are so effective. At times, you might actually be able to feel the physical changes happening in your brain as you develop this new knowledge and these new skills. That doesn't come about without effort.

The important thing to remember is that while active revision feels much more like hard work than passive revision, you don't actually need to do nearly as much of it. That's because you remember knowledge and skills when you use active revision. When you use passive revision, it is much, much harder for the knowledge and skills to stick in your memory.

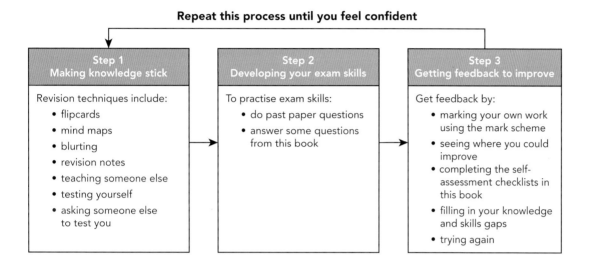

Repeat this process until you feel confident

Step 1
Making knowledge stick

Revision techniques include:
- flipcards
- mind maps
- blurting
- revision notes
- teaching someone else
- testing yourself
- asking someone else to test you

Step 2
Developing your exam skills

To practise exam skills:
- do past paper questions
- answer some questions from this book

Step 3
Getting feedback to improve

Get feedback by:
- marking your own work using the mark scheme
- seeing where you could improve
- completing the self-assessment checklists in this book
- filling in your knowledge and skills gaps
- trying again

How to improve your exam skills

This book helps you to improve in eight different areas of exam skills, which are divided across three categories. These skills are highlighted in this book in the Exam skills focus at the start of each chapter and developed throughout the book using targeted questions, advice and reflections.

1   **Understand the questions: what are you being asked to do?**

- Know your question types.

- Understand command words.

- Work with mark scheme awareness.

2   **How to answer questions brilliantly**

- Understand connections between concepts.

- Keep to time.

- Know what a good answer looks like.

3   **Give yourself the best chance of success**

- Reflect on progress.

- Know how to manage test anxiety.

Understand the questions: what are you being asked to do?

Know your question types

In any exam, there will be a range of different question types. These different question types will test different types of thinking skills from Bloom's Taxonomy.

It is very important that you learn to recognise different question types. If you do lots of past papers, over time you will begin to recognise the structure of the paper for each of your subjects. You will know which types of questions may come first and which ones are more likely to come at the end of the paper. You can also complete past paper questions in the Exam practice sections in this book for additional practice.

You will also recognise the differences between questions worth a lower number of marks and questions worth more marks. The key differences are:

- how much you will need to write in your answer
- how sophisticated your answer needs to be in terms of the detail you give and the depth of thinking you show.

Types of questions

1 **Multiple choice questions**

Multiple choice questions are generally worth smaller numbers of marks. You will be given several possible answers to the question, and you will have to work out which one is correct using your knowledge and skills.

There is a chance of you getting the right answer with multiple choice questions even if you don't know the answer. This is why you must **always give an answer for multiple choice questions** as it means there is a chance you will earn the mark.

Multiple choice questions are often harder than they appear. The possible answers can be very similar to each other. This means you must be confident in how you work out answers or have a high level of understanding to tell the difference between the possible answers.

Being confident in your subject knowledge and doing lots of practice multiple choice questions will set you up for success. Use the resources in this book and the accompanying online resources to build your confidence.

This example of a multiple choice question is worth one mark. You can see that all the answers have one part in common with at least one other answer. For example, palisade cells is included in three of the possible answers. That's why you have to really know the detail of your content knowledge to do well with multiple choice questions.

Which two types of cells are found in plant leaves?

A Palisade mesophyll and stomata
B Palisade mesophyll and root hair
C Stomata and chloroplast
D Chloroplast and palisade mesophyll

2 Questions requiring longer-form answers

Questions requiring longer-form answers need you to write out your answer yourself.

With these questions, take careful note of how many marks are available and how much space you've been given for your answer. These two things will give you a good idea about how much you should say and how much time you should spend on the question.

A rough rule to follow is to write one sentence, or make one point, for each mark that is available. You will get better and better at these longer-form questions the more you practise them.

In this example of a history question, you can see it is worth four marks. It is not asking for an explanation, just for you to list Lloyd George's aims. Therefore, you need to make four correct points in order to get full marks.

What were Lloyd George's aims during negotiations leading to the Treaty of Versailles?   [4]

3 Essay questions

Essay questions are the longest questions you will be asked to answer in an exam. They examine the higher-order thinking skills from Bloom's Taxonomy such as analysis, synthesis and evaluation.

To do well in essay questions, you need to talk about what you know, giving your opinion, comparing one concept or example to another, and evaluating your own ideas or the ones you're discussing in your answer.

You also need to have a strong structure and logical argument that guides the reader through your thought process. This usually means having an introduction, some main body paragraphs that discuss one point at a time, and a conclusion.

Essay questions are usually level-marked. This means that you don't get one mark per point you make. Instead, you're given marks for the quality of the ideas you're sharing as well as how well you present those ideas through the subject-specific language you use and the structure of your essay.

Practising essays and becoming familiar with the mark scheme is the only way to get really good at them.

Understand command words

What are command words?

Command words are the most important words in every exam question. This is because command words tell you what you need to do in your answer. Do you remember Bloom's Taxonomy? Command words tell you which thinking skill you need to demonstrate in the answer to each question.

Two very common command words are **describe** and **explain**.

When you see the command word 'describe' in a question, you're being asked to show lower-order thinking skills like knowledge and understanding. The question will either be worth fewer marks, or you will need to make more points if it is worth more marks.

The command word 'explain' is asking you to show higher-order thinking skills. When you see the command word 'explain', you need to be able to say how or why something happens.

You need to understand all of the relevant command words for the subjects you are taking. Ask your teacher where to find them if you are not sure. It's best not to try to memorise the list of command words, but to become familiar with what command words are asking for by doing lots of practice questions and marking your own work.

How to work with command words

When you first see an exam question, read it through once. Then, read it through again and identify the command word(s). Underline the command word(s) to make it clear to yourself which they are every time you refer back to the question.

You may also want to identify the **content** words in the question and underline them with a different colour. Content words tell you which area of knowledge you need to draw on to answer the question.

In this example, command words are shown in red and content words in blue:

1 a Explain **four** reasons why governments might support business start-ups. [8]

Adapted from Cambridge IGCSE Business Studies (0450)
Q1a Paper 21 June 2022

Marking your own work using the mark scheme will help you get even better at understanding command words and knowing how to give good answers for each.

Work with mark scheme awareness

The most transformative thing that any student can do to improve their marks is to work with mark schemes. This means using mark schemes to mark your own work at every opportunity.

Many students are very nervous about marking their own work as they do not feel experienced or qualified enough. However, being brave enough to try to mark your own work and taking the time to get good at it will improve your marks hugely.

Why marking your own work makes such a big difference

Marking your own work can help you to improve your answers in the following ways:

1 Answering the question

Having a deep and detailed understanding of what is required by the question enables you to answer the question more clearly and more accurately.

It can also help you to give the required information using fewer words and in less time, as you can avoid including unrelated points or topics in your answer.

2 Using subject-specific vocabulary

Every subject has subject-specific vocabulary. This includes technical terms for objects or concepts in a subject, such as mitosis and meiosis in biology. It also includes how you talk about the subject, using appropriate vocabulary that may differ from everyday language. For example, in any science subject you might be asked to describe the trend on a graph.

Your answer could say it 'goes up fast' or your answer could say it 'increases rapidly'. You would not get marks for saying 'it goes up fast', but you would for saying it 'increases rapidly'. This is the difference between everyday language and formal scientific language.

When you answer lots of practice questions, you become fluent in the language specific to your subject.

3 Knowing how much to write

It's very common for students to either write too much or too little to answer questions. Becoming familiar with the mark schemes for many different questions will help you to gain a better understanding of how much you need to write in order to get a good mark.

4 Structuring your answer

There are often clues in questions about how to structure your answer. However, mark schemes give you an even stronger idea of the structure you should use in your answers.

For example, if a question says:

'Describe and explain two reasons why…'

You can give a clear answer by:

- Describing reason 1

- Explaining reason 1

- Describing reason 2

- Explaining reason 2

Having a very clear structure will also make it easier to identify where you have earned marks. This means that you're more likely to be awarded the number of marks you deserve.

5 Keeping to time

Answering the question, using subject-specific vocabulary, knowing how much to write and giving a clear structure to your answer will all help you to keep to time in an exam. You will not waste time by writing too much for any answer. Therefore, you will have sufficient time to give a good answer to every question.

How to answer exam questions brilliantly

Understand connections between concepts

One of the higher-level thinking skills in Bloom's Taxonomy is **synthesis**. Synthesis means making connections between different areas of knowledge. You may have heard about synoptic links. Making synoptic links is the same as showing the thinking skill of synthesis.

Exam questions that ask you to show your synthesis skills are usually worth the highest number of marks on an exam paper. To write good answers to these questions, you need to spend time thinking about the links between the topics you've studied **before** you arrive in your exam. A great way of doing this is using mind maps.

How to create a mind map

To create a mind map:

1   Use a large piece of paper and several different coloured pens.

2   Write the name of your subject in the middle. Then, write the key topic areas evenly spaced around the edge, each with a different colour.

3   Then, around each topic area, start to write the detail of what you can remember. If you find something that is connected with something you studied in another topic, you can draw a line linking the two things together.

This is a good way of practising your retrieval of information as well as linking topics together.

Answering synoptic exam questions

You will recognise questions that require you to make links between concepts because they have a higher number of marks. You will have practised them using this book and the accompanying resources.

To answer a synoptic exam question:

1   **Identify the command and content words.** You are more likely to find command words like **discuss** and **explain** in these questions. They might also have phrases like 'the connection between'.

2   **Make a plan for your answer.** It is worth taking a short amount of time to think about what you're going to write in your answer. Think carefully about what information you're going to put in, the links between the different pieces of information and how you're going to structure your answer to make your ideas clear.

3   **Use linking words and phrases in your answer.** For example, 'therefore', 'because', due to', 'since' or 'this means that'.

Here is an example of an English Literature exam question that requires you to make synoptic links in your answer.

1   Discuss Carol Ann Duffy's exploration of childhood in her poetry.
     Refer to two poems in your answer.   [25]

Content words are shown in blue; command words are shown in red.

This question is asking you to explore the theme of childhood in Duffy's poetry. You need to choose two of her poems to refer to in your answer. This means you need a good knowledge of her poetry, and to be familiar with her exploration of childhood, so that you can easily select two poems that will give you plenty to say in your answer.

Keep to time

Managing your time in exams is really important. Some students do not achieve to the best of their abilities because they run out of time to answer all the questions. However, if you manage your time well, you will be able to attempt every question on the exam paper.

Why is it important to attempt all the questions on an exam paper?

If you attempt every question on a paper, you have the best chance of achieving the highest mark you are capable of.

Students who manage their time poorly in exams will often spend far too long on some questions and not even attempt others. Most students are unlikely to get full marks on many questions, but you will get zero marks for the questions you don't answer. You can maximise your marks by giving an answer to every question.

Minutes per mark

The most important way to keep to time is knowing how many minutes you can spend on each mark.

For example, if your exam paper has 90 marks available and you have 90 minutes, you know there is 1 mark per minute.

Therefore, if you have a five-mark question, you should spend five minutes on it.

Sometimes, you can give a good answer in less time than you have budgeted using the minutes per mark technique. If this happens, you will have more time to spend on questions that use higher-order thinking skills, or more time on checking your work.

How to get faster at answering exam questions

The best way to get faster at answering exam questions is to do lots of practice. You should practise each question type that will be in your exam, marking your own work, so that you know precisely how that question works and what is required by the question. Use the questions in this book to get better and better at answering each question type.

Use the 'Slow, Slow, Quick' technique to get faster.

Take your time answering questions when you first start practising them. You may answer them with the support of the coursebook, your notes or the mark scheme. These things will support you with your content knowledge, the language you use in your answer and the structure of your answer.

Every time you practise this question type, you will get more confident and faster. You will become experienced with this question type, so that it is easy for you to recall the subject knowledge and write it down using the correct language and a good structure.

Calculating marks per minute

Use this calculation to work out how long you have for each mark:

total time in the exam / number of marks available = minutes per mark

Calculate how long you have for a question worth more than one mark like this:

minutes per mark $\times$ marks available for this question = number of minutes for this question

What about time to check your work?

It is a very good idea to check your work at the end of an exam. You need to work out if this is feasible with the minutes per mark available to you. If you're always rushing to finish the questions, you shouldn't budget checking time. However, if you usually have time to spare, then you can budget checking time.

To include checking time in your minutes per mark calculation:

(total time in the exam – checking time) / number of marks available = minutes per mark

Know what a good answer looks like

It is much easier to give a good answer if you know what a good answer looks like.

Use these methods to know what a good answer looks like.

1   **Sample answers** – you can find sample answers in these places:

- from your teacher

- written by your friends or other members of your class

- in this book.

2   **Look at mark schemes** – mark schemes are full of information about what you should include in your answers. Get familiar with mark schemes to gain a better understanding of the type of things a good answer would contain.

3   **Feedback from your teacher** – if you are finding it difficult to improve your exam skills for a particular type of question, ask your teacher for detailed feedback. You should also look at their comments on your work in detail.

Give yourself the best chance of success

Reflection on progress

As you prepare for your exam, it's important to reflect on your progress. Taking time to think about what you're doing well and what could be improved brings more focus to your revision. Reflecting on progress also helps you to continuously improve your knowledge and exam skills.

How do you reflect on progress?

Use the 'Reflection' feature in this book to help you reflect on your progress during your exam preparation. Then, at the end of each revision session, take a few minutes to think about the following:

	What went well? What would you do the same next time?	What didn't go well? What would you do differently next time?
Your subject knowledge		
How you revised your subject knowledge – did you use active retrieval techniques?		
Your use of subject-specific and academic language		
Understanding the question by identifying command words and content words		
Giving a clear structure to your answer		
Keeping to time		
Marking your own work		

Remember to check for silly mistakes – things like missing out the units after you carefully calculated your answer.

Use the mark scheme to mark your own work. Every time you mark your own work, you will be recognising the good and bad aspects of your work, so that you can progressively give better answers over time.

When do you need to come back to this topic or skill?

Earlier in this section of the book, we talked about revision skills and the importance of spaced retrieval. When you reflect on your progress, you need to think about how soon you need to return to the topic or skill you've just been focusing on.

For example, if you were really disappointed with your subject knowledge, it would be a good idea to do some more active retrieval and practice questions on this topic tomorrow. However, if you did really well you can feel confident you know this topic and come back to it again in three weeks' or a month's time.

The same goes for exam skills. If you were disappointed with how you answered the question, you should look at some sample answers and try this type of question again soon. However, if you did well, you can move on to other types of exam questions.

Improving your memory of subject knowledge

Sometimes students slip back into using passive revision techniques, such as only reading the coursebook or their notes, rather than also using active revision techniques, like testing themselves using flip cards or blurting.

You can avoid this mistake by observing how well your learning is working as you revise. You should be thinking to yourself, 'Am I remembering this? Am I understanding this? Is this revision working?'

If the answer to any of those questions is 'no', then you need to change what you're doing to revise this particular topic. For example, if you don't understand, you could look up your topic in a different textbook in the school library to see if a different explanation helps. Or you could see if you can find a video online that brings the idea to life.

You are in control

When you're studying for exams it's easy to think that your teachers are in charge. However, you have to remember that you are studying for your exams and the results you get will be yours and no one else's.

That means you have to take responsibility for all your exam preparation. You have the power to change how you're preparing if what you're doing isn't working. You also have control over what you revise and when: you can make sure you focus on your weaker topics and skills to improve your achievement in the subject.

This isn't always easy to do. Sometimes you have to find an inner ability that you have not used before. But, if you are determined enough to do well, you can find what it takes to focus, improve and keep going.

What is test anxiety?

Do you get worried or anxious about exams? Does your worry or anxiety impact how well you do in tests and exams?

Test anxiety is part of your natural stress response.

The stress response evolved in animals and humans many thousands of years ago to help keep them alive. Let's look at an example.

The stress response in the wild

Imagine an impala grazing in the grasslands of East Africa. It's happily and calmly eating grass in its herd in what we would call the parasympathetic state of rest and repair.

Then the impala sees a lion. The impala suddenly panics because its life is in danger. This state of panic is also known as the stressed or sympathetic state. The sympathetic state presents itself in three forms: flight, fight and freeze.

The impala starts to run away from the lion. Running away is known as the flight stress response.

The impala might not be fast enough to run away from the lion. The lion catches it but has a loose grip. The impala struggles to try to get away. This struggle is the fight stress response.

However, the lion gets an even stronger grip on the impala. Now the only chance of the impala surviving is playing dead. The impala goes limp, its heart rate and breathing slow down. This is called the freeze stress response. The lion believes that it has killed the impala so it drops the impala to the ground. Now the impala can switch back into the flight response and run away.

The impala is now safe – the different stages of the stress response have saved its life.

What has the impala got to do with your exams?

When you feel test anxiety, you have the same physiological stress responses as an impala being hunted by a lion. Unfortunately, the human nervous system cannot tell the difference between a life-threatening situation, such as being chased by a lion, and the stress of taking an exam.

If you understand how the stress response works in the human nervous system, you will be able to learn techniques to reduce test anxiety.

The role of the vagus nerve in test anxiety

The vagus nerve is the part of your nervous system that determines your stress response. Vagus means 'wandering' in Latin, so the vagus nerve is also known as the 'wandering nerve'. The vagus nerve wanders from your brain, down each side of your body, to nearly all your organs, including your lungs, heart, kidneys, liver, digestive system and bladder.

If you are in a stressful situation, like an exam, your vagus nerve sends a message to all these different organs to activate their stress response. Here are some common examples:

* **Heart** beats faster.

* **Kidneys** produce more adrenaline so that you can run, making you fidgety and distracted.

* **Digestive system** and **bladder** want to eliminate all waste products so that energy can be used for fight or flight.

If you want to feel calmer about your revision and exams, you need to do two things to help you move into the parasympathetic, or rest and repair, state:

1 Work with your vagus nerve to send messages of safety through your body.

2 Change your perception of the test so that you see it as safe and not dangerous.

How to cope with test anxiety

1 Be well prepared

Good preparation is the most important part of managing test anxiety. The better your preparation, the more confident you will be. If you are confident, you will not perceive the test or exam as dangerous, so the sympathetic nervous system responses of fight, flight and freeze are less likely to happen.

This book is all about helping you to be well prepared and building your confidence in your knowledge and ability to answer exam questions well. Working through the knowledge recall questions will help you to become more confident in your knowledge of the subject. The practice questions and exam skills questions will help you to become more confident in communicating your knowledge in an exam.

To be well prepared, look at the advice in the rest of this chapter and use it as you work through the questions in this book.

2 Work with your vagus nerve

The easiest way to work with your vagus nerve to tell it that you're in a safe situation is through your breathing. This means breathing deeply into the bottom of your lungs, so that your stomach expands, and then breathing out for longer than you breathed in. You can do this with counting.

Breathe in deeply, expanding your abdomen, for the count of four; breathe out, drawing your navel back towards your spine, for the count of five, six or seven. Repeat this at least three times. However, you can do it for as long as it takes for you to feel calm.

The important thing is that you breathe out for longer than you breathe in. This is because when you breathe in, your heart rate increases slightly, and when you breathe out, your heart rate decreases slightly. If you're spending more time breathing out overall, you will be decreasing your heart rate over time.

3 Feel it

Anxiety is an uncomfortable, difficult thing to feel. That means that many people try to run away from anxious feelings. However, this means the stress just gets stored in your body for you to feel later.

When you feel anxious, follow these four steps:

1 Pause.

2 Place one hand on your heart and one hand on your stomach.

3 Notice what you're feeling.

4 Stay with your feelings.

What you will find is that if you are willing to experience what you feel for a minute or two, the feeling of anxiety will usually pass very quickly.

4 Write or talk it out

If your thoughts are moving very quickly, it is often better to get them out of your mind and on to paper.

You could take a few minutes to write down everything that comes through your mind, then rip up your paper and throw it away. If you don't like writing, you can speak aloud alone or to someone you trust.

Other ways to break the stress cycle

Exercise and movement	Being friendly	Laughter
• Run or walk. • Dance. • Lift weights. • Yoga. Anything that involves moving your body is helpful.	• Chat to someone in your study break. • Talk to the cashier when you buy your lunch.	• Watch or listen to a funny show on TV or online. • Talk with someone who makes you laugh. • Look at photos of fun times.
Have a hug	Releasing emotions	Creativity
• Hug a friend or relative. • Cuddle a pet e.g. a cat. Hug for 20 seconds or until you feel calm and relaxed.	It is healthy to release negative or sad emotions. Crying is often a quick way to get rid of these difficult feelings so if you feel like you need to cry, allow it.	• Paint, draw or sketch. • Sew, knit or crochet. • Cook, build something.

If you have long-term symptoms of anxiety, it is important to tell someone you trust and ask for help.

Your perfect revision session

1 Intention

What do you want to achieve in this revision session?

- Choose an area of knowledge or an exam skill that you want to focus on.
- Choose some questions from this book that focus on this knowledge area or skill.
- Gather any other resources you will need e.g. pen, paper, flashcards, coursebook.

2 Focus

Set your focus for the session

- Remove distractions from your study area e.g. leave your phone in another room.
- Write down on a piece of paper or sticky note the knowledge area or skill you're intending to focus on.
- Close your eyes and take three deep breaths, with the exhale longer than the inhale.

3 Revision

Revise your knowledge and understanding

- To improve your knowledge and understanding of the topic, use your coursebook, notes or flashcards, including active learning techniques.
- To improve your exam skills, look at previous answers, teacher feedback, mark schemes, sample answers or examiners' reports.

4 Practice

Answer practice questions

- Use the questions in this book, or in the additional online resources, to practise your exam skills.
- If the exam is soon, do this in timed conditions without the support of the coursebook or your notes.
- If the exam is a long time away, you can use your notes and resources to help you.

5 Feedback

Mark your answers

- Use mark schemes to mark your work.
- Reflect on what you've done well and what you could do to improve next time.

6 Next steps

What have you learned about your progress from this revision session? What do you need to do next?

- What did you do well? Feel good about these things, and know it's safe to set these things aside for a while.
- What do you need to work on? How are you going to improve? Make a plan to get better at the things you didn't do well or didn't know.

7 Rest

Take a break

- Do something completely different to rest: get up, move or do something creative or practical.
- Remember that rest is an important part of studying, as it gives your brain a chance to integrate your learning.

1 Cell structure

KNOWLEDGE FOCUS

In this chapter you will answer questions on:

- cells
- cell biology and microscopy
- plant and animal cells as seen with a light microscope
- measuring size and calculating magnification
- electron microscopy
- plant and animal cells as seen with an electron microscope
- bacteria
- comparing prokaryotic cells with eukaryotic cells
- viruses.

EXAM SKILLS FOCUS

In this chapter you will:

- show that you understand the command words 'identify' and 'calculate' and can answer 'identify' and 'calculate' questions.

Command words are the words used in exam questions that let you know what is expected in your answer. It is important that you are familiar with the command words in the syllabus, and understand what each command word is instructing you to do. In this chapter, look out for the command words 'identify' and 'calculate'. The definitions for these command words are given below.

Identify	name/select/recognise
Calculate	work out from given facts, figures or information

'Identify' questions often ask you to name or recognise information from a diagram or a graph, or make a decision about the location or name of a particular biological process or structure. You might be asked to draw a label line or a cross on a diagram. When you answer the 'identify' questions in this chapter, be clear in your responses and try to spell key terms correctly.

For 'calculate' questions that are not multiple choice you must show all the steps you used to work out the answer, using the correct units from the information in the question. You may be given marks for using the right method even if your final answer is incorrect. Practise showing all your working as you answer the 'calculate' questions in this chapter.

1.1 Cells are the basic units of life

1 Eukaryotic cells contain an organelle that is absent from prokaryotic cells. What is the name of this organelle and what does it contain?

2 Identify the correct statement about a eukaryotic cell.

   A Eukaryotic cells have no membrane-bound nuclei.
   B Prokaryotic cells evolved from eukaryotic cells.
   C Eukaryotic cells include animals, plants, fungi and some other organisms.
   D Eukaryotic cells contain fewer different organelles than prokaryotic cells. **[Total: 1]**

> **UNDERSTAND THESE TERMS**
> - cell
> - organelle
> - eukaryotes
> - prokaryotes

1.2 Cell biology and microscopy

1 What are the two main different types of microscope? Explain how they are different.

2 Calculate how many millimetres there are in 2.3 nanometres.

   A 2300 mm
   B 2 300 000 mm
   C 0.0023 mm
   D 0.000 0023 mm **[Total: 1]**

3 Give the answer to question **2** in standard form. **[Total: 1]**

1.3 Plant and animal cells as seen with a light microscope

1   Copy and complete the table:

Organelles seen with a light microscope	Function
cell surface membrane	
nucleus	
mitochondrion	
Golgi body	
cell wall	
large permanent vacuole	
chloroplast	

UNDERSTAND
THESE TERMS

• chromatin

• nucleolus

• tonoplast

2   Name the organelles found in plant cells that are not found
in animal cells.   [Total: 1]

3   Describe the structure and role of the plasmodesmata in plant cells.   [Total: 3]

1.4 Measuring size and calculating magnification

1   What is the formula for working out the magnification of an image?

2   Figure 1.1 shows a micrograph of plant cells. The actual length of the cell between
points **a** and **b** on the line is 12 μm. The length of the line between **a** and **b**
on the diagram is 3 mm. Calculate the magnification of this image.   [Total: 2]

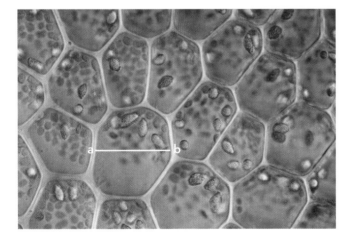

Figure 1.1

3 Figure 1.2 shows three fields of view seen using a high-power (×40) objective lens: **a** an eyepiece graticule scale; **b** human cheek epithelial cells and the eyepiece graticule scale; **c** the eyepiece graticule scale and the stage micrometer scale. Calibrate the eyepiece graticule to then calculate the actual diameter of the cell shown on the eyepiece graticule. **[Total: 3]**

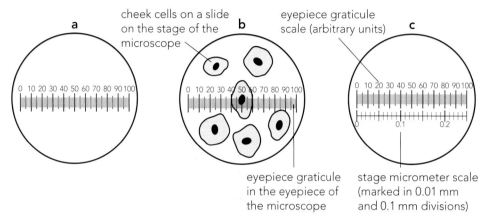

Figure 1.2

UNDERSTAND THESE TERMS

- magnification
- eyepiece graticule
- stage micrometer
- micrograph

1.5 Electron microscopy

1 Why do electron microscopes have a higher resolution than light microscopes?

2 There are two types of electron microscopes: transmission and scanning. Draw a table. Put each statement into the correct column to indicate whether the feature is for a transmission or a scanning electron microscope.

Statements

- The beam of electrons passes through the specimen.
- The beam of electrons reflects off some parts of the specimen.
- Thin sections of a specimen are used.
- Fine internal details of cells can be seen.
- A 3D image is created.

3 Describe the main differences between a light microscope and an electron microscope. **[Total: 4]**

UNDERSTAND THIS TERM

- resolution

1.6 Plant and animal cells as seen with an electron microscope

1 Figure 1.3 shows organelles on a transmission electron micrograph of part of a cell from the pancreas. Use the list provided to identify parts **A–D**.

> nucleus   nuclear envelope   mitochondrion
> rough endoplasmic reticulum

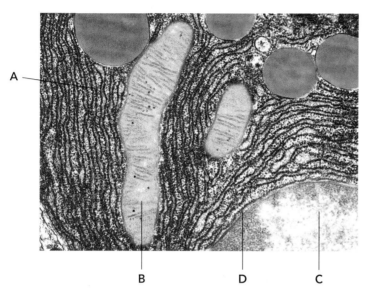

A

B   D   C

Figure 1.3: A transmission electron micrograph of a part of a cell from the pancreas

2 How does the structure of a mitochondrion link to its function?

3 State the name of three organelles that are visible with an electron microscope and that are not visible using a light microscope.   [Total: 3]

4 Which statement about centrioles is correct?

   A   Centrioles are formed from microtubules
   B   Centrioles are only found in plant cells
   C   Centrioles are found in the nucleus
   D   Centrioles are involved in the synthesis of ATP   [Total: 1]

5 State one function of cilia found in epithelial cells in the airways of mammals.   [Total: 1]

1.7 Bacteria

1   What is the main component of bacterial cell walls?

2   Identify the organelles labelled **A–D** in Figure 1.4.

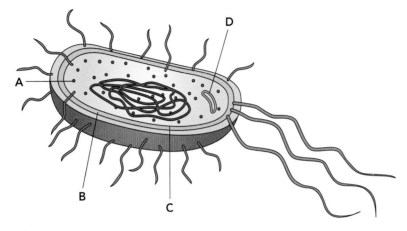

Figure 1.4: A bacterial cell

3   Which statements are correct about bacteria?

   A   Bacterial cells contain circular DNA

   B   Bacterial cells contain a nuclear envelope

   C   Bacterial cells contain 70S ribosomes

   D   Bacterial cells contain mitochondria   **[Total: 2]**

UNDERSTAND THESE TERMS
• peptidoglycan
• plasmid

1.8 Comparing prokaryotic cells with eukaryotic cells

1   List the organelles that are only found in eukaryotic cells.

2   Describe the similarities and differences between the structure of a prokaryotic cell and the structure of a eukaryotic cell.   **[Total: 5]**

REFLECTION

How did you do on question **2**? It asks for similarities and differences, so you have to state the feature in the prokaryotic cell and the different feature in the eukaryotic cell, and not just state one or the other. (For example saying prokaryotic cells are much smaller than eukaryotic cells, and not just saying prokaryotic cells are small.) A good way to ensure this is to always include the word 'whereas' in your sentence.

1.9 Viruses

1   Put the following into size order (from smallest to largest): eukaryotic cells, viruses, prokaryotic cells.

2   Some viruses have an outer envelope. State the molecule that is the main component of the outer envelope.   **[Total: 1]**

3   Identify which option correctly states the two structures that all viruses consist of.

   A   DNA/RNA and a cell surface membrane

   B   DNA/RNA and a cell wall

   C   a protein capsid and a cell surface membrane

   D   a protein capsid and DNA/RNA   **[Total: 1]**

SELF-ASSESSMENT CHECKLIST

Let's revisit the Knowledge focus and Exam skills focus for this chapter.

Decide how confident you are with each statement.

Now I can:	Show it	Needs more work	Almost there	Confident to move on
explain that cells are the basic units of life	State the cell structures of eukaryotic cells.			
use the units of measurement relevant to microscopy	Convert measurements to the same units within microscopy calculations.			
recognise the common structures found in cells as seen with a light microscope and outline their structures and functions	Create a table outlining the organelle names, structure and functions.			
compare the key structural features of animal and plant cells	Draw and label an animal and a plant cell, highlighting any organelles found only in a plant cell.			
use a light microscope and make temporary preparations to observe cells	Complete the microscopy required practical and draw your observations.			
recognise, draw and measure cell structures from temporary preparations and micrographs	Label organelles on a micrograph of an animal and a plant cell.			
calculate magnifications of images and actual sizes of specimens using drawings or micrographs	Find a micrograph on the internet and calculate the viewing magnification on the screen from the scale bar and the actual size of the image.			

CONTINUED

Now I can:	Show it	Needs more work	Almost there	Confident to move on
explain the use of the electron microscope to study cells with reference to the increased resolution of electron microscopes	Define the term 'resolution' and explain why electron microscopes have a higher resolution.			
recognise the common structures found in cells as seen with an electron microscope and outline their structures and functions	Identify the structures only visible with a light microscope and explain how their structure links to their function.			
outline briefly the role of ATP in cells	Give one use of ATP within a cell.			
describe the structure of bacteria and compare the structure of prokaryotic cells with eukaryotic cells	Create a table to identify the differences between a prokaryotic and eukaryotic cell.			
describe the structure of viruses	State the two structural features all viruses have.			
show that I understand the command words 'identify' and 'calculate' and can answer 'identify' and 'calculate' questions	Explain to someone what the command words 'identify' and 'calculate' mean and write an example question for each, along with their mark schemes.			

2 Biological molecules

In this chapter you will practise answering 'describe' questions. The definition of this command word is given below.

Describe	state the points of a topic/give characteristics and main features

In this topic you may be asked to describe the main features of biochemical tests, or the structure of different biological molecules such as fats and carbohydrates. Make sure you include the main features in your answer. This will help ensure you are more concise with your answers.

2.1 Biochemistry and
2.2 The building blocks of life

1   The building blocks of life are simple biological molecules that join together to form larger, more complex molecules. Match up the larger molecules in column A with the building blocks they are formed of (column B).

A
Polysaccharides
Nucleic acids
Proteins
Lipids

B
Amino acids
Nucleotides
Monosaccharides
Fatty acids and glycerol

2   Give the name of one element that all organic molecules contain.   **[Total: 1]**

2.3 Monomers, polymers and macromolecules

1   What does the term 'poly' refer to in polysaccharide, polynucleotide and polypeptide?

2   There are three types of giant molecules in living organisms, polysaccharides, polynucleotides and polypeptides.

   a   State the term given to a large molecule.   [1]

   b   Describe a condensation reaction, which is required to make these giant molecules.   [2]

                                                      [Total: 3]

UNDERSTAND THESE TERMS
• macromolecule
• polymer
• monomer
• condensation reaction
• hydrolysis

2.4 Carbohydrates

1   Draw the ring structure for α-glucose and β-glucose.

2   Describe the molecular structure of starch.   **[Total: 3]**

3   Starch is composed of the monosaccharide glucose.
Describe the reaction that joins α-glucose monomers together and state the bond that is formed.   **[Total: 3]**

4 Figure 2.1 shows the structure of a molecule of maltose.

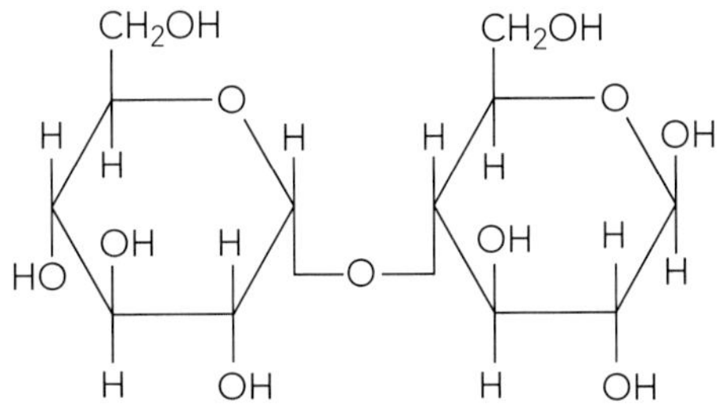

Figure 2.1

a State the monosaccharides maltose is made of. [1]

b On a copy of Figure 2.1, sketch a box around the glycosidic bond. [1]

[Total: 2]

UNDERSTAND THESE TERMS

- monosaccharide
- disaccharide
- polysaccharides
- glycosidic bond
- hydrogen bond

« RECALL AND CONNECT 1 «

Look back at Chapter 1 Cell structure: Describe the structure of a virus.

2.5 Lipids

1 Which diagram from Figure 2.2 shows the structure of a saturated fatty acid?

A

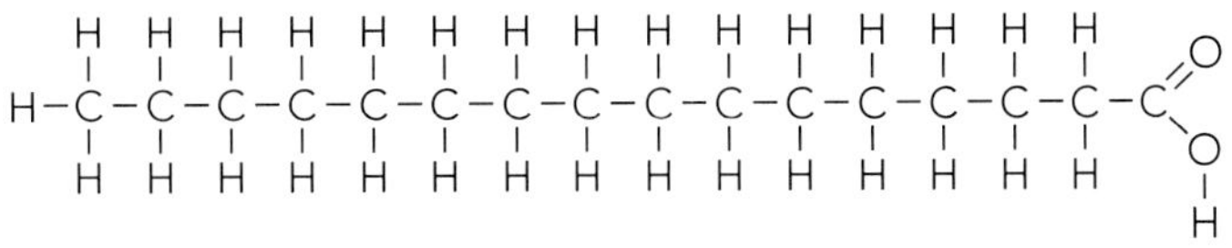

B

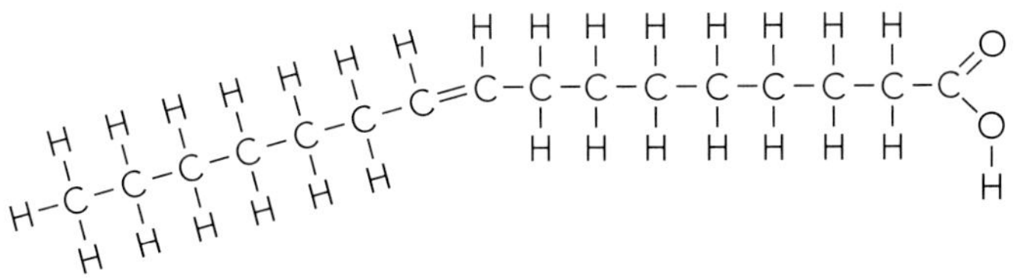

Figure 2.2: Diagrams of a saturated and an unsaturated fatty acid

2 Copy and complete the paragraph below by filling in the blanks.

Triglycerides are composed of fatty acids. All fatty acids contain the acidic .... group, which forms the 'top' of the fatty acid. The 'tail' of the fatty acid is made up of a long chain containing .... and .... (a hydrocarbon). If a fatty acid tail has at least one double bond between the carbon atoms (C=C) it is classed as .... Whereas, if the fatty acid tail contains only single bonds between the carbon atoms (C–C) it is classed as ....

UNDERSTAND THESE TERMS

• ester bond/ester linkage

• triglycerides

3 Which of the statements are true and which are false?

a Triglycerides make excellent energy stores.

b Phospholipids are stored just below the skin.

c The phosphate group in the head of a phospholipid makes it hydrophilic.

4 Figure 2.3 shows a triglyceride molecule.

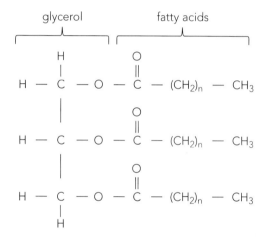

Figure 2.3

a Identify one of the ester bonds in Figure 2.3 by copying the figure then drawing around an ester bond. [1]

b State the name of the reaction that joined the glycerol and fatty acids together. [1]

c Describe the biochemical test for a lipid. [3]

[Total: 5]

REFLECTION

How confident are you that you understand the command word 'describe'? Did you state each part of the biochemical test for the lipid? Using flashcards for the methods of each biochemical test can help you to remember all the points to include.

2.6 Proteins

1 The primary structure of a protein is the unique sequence of amino acids, which determines the location of the bonds in the tertiary structure.

    a   How many different naturally occurring amino acids are commonly found in proteins?

    b   What are the four bonds that help to keep proteins folded in the tertiary structure?

2 Describe the protein structure of haemoglobin.   **[Total: 3]**

3 Sketch the general structure of an amino acid.   **[Total: 2]**

4   a   Describe the structure of a collagen molecule.   [4]

    b   Describe how the arrangement of collagen molecules in a collagen fibre relates to its function.   [3]

                                                   [Total: 7]

> **UNDERSTAND THESE TERMS**
>
> - primary structure
> - secondary structure
> - tertiary structure
> - quaternary structure

≪ RECALL AND CONNECT 2 ≪

Look back at Chapter 1 Cell structure: Describe the structure and function of ribosomes in eukaryotic cells.

2.7 Water

1 Which property of water results in each of the following important roles in organisms?

    a   The transport of sucrose as part of the phloem of plants.

    b   The cooling of plants when they transpire.

    c   The cooling of mammals when they sweat.

2 Copy and complete the summary table for water.

Property	Description of property	Importance/role in organisms
Solvent action	Water is an excellent solvent for ions and polar molecules because it has uneven charge distribution, so water is attracted to and surrounds the ions.	Ions will dissolve in the cytoplasm, blood and lymph so they can be transported around. In plants, ions will dissolve in water and can then be transported around in the xylem and phloem.
High specific heat capacity		
High latent heat of vapourisation		

3   Water is one of the most important biochemicals to organisms as, despite its simple structure, it has many important functions.

    a   Describe how the structure of water results in high latent heat of vapourisation. [2]

    b   Suggest how sweating helps to lower body temperature. [3]

[Total: 5]

REFLECTION

How did you find the water summary table task? Did you remember all the descriptions of the properties of water? If you struggled to remember any of the descriptions, consider how you consolidated those facts into your memory and whether this was effective. Repeatedly testing your knowledge spaced out over time will improve your long-term memory of the facts, which will help improve your confidence and speed in the exam, and therefore your overall grade.

SELF-ASSESSMENT CHECKLIST

Let's revisit the Knowledge focus and Exam skills focus for this chapter.

Decide how confident you are with each statement.

Now I can	Show it	Needs more work	Almost there	Confident to move on
describe how large biological molecules are made from smaller molecules	Describe a condensation reaction.			
describe the structure of carbohydrates, lipids and proteins and how their structure relates to their functions	Describe the structure of cellulose and explain how this structure relates to its function.			
describe and carry out biochemical tests to identify carbohydrates, lipids and proteins	Describe the test for reducing sugars.			
explain some key properties of water that make life possible	State one property of water and explain how it is important to organisms.			
show that I understand the 'describe' command word and can answer 'describe' questions	Answer the 'describe' question in Exam practice 1, making sure that your answer states the points of the topic/gives characteristics and main features.			

Exam practice 1

This section contains past paper questions from previous Cambridge exams, which draw together your knowledge on a range of topics that you have covered up to this point. These questions give you the opportunity to test your knowledge and understanding. Additional past paper practice questions can be found in the accompanying digital material.

The following question has an example student response and commentary provided. Work through the question first, then compare your answer to the sample response and commentary. Are your answers different to the sample responses?

1   Picornaviruses are small viruses that are 30 nm in diameter. Picornaviruses are able to enter the cells of mammals and birds and can replicate within these cells. Fig. 1.1 shows the entry of a picornavirus into its host cell.

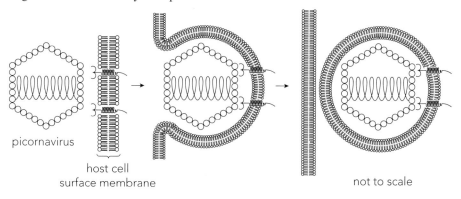

picornavirus

host cell
surface membrane

not to scale

Fig. 1.1

a   State the key features of a virus, such as picornavirus.   [2]

b   State, with reasons, whether a picornavirus can be seen using the light microscope.   [3]

c   With reference to Fig. 1.1, describe how the picornavirus enters the host cell.   [3]

[Total: 8]

Cambridge International AS & A Level Biology (9700) Paper 22, Q1, June 2020

Example student response	Commentary
1 a Capsid and DNA	These answers are both correct. The student could have also said protein coat (instead of capsid). Instead of DNA, the student could have also said RNA or nucleic acid core. *This answer is awarded 2 out of 2 marks.*
b No, because they are too small to be seen with a light microscope.	The student has the correct idea here, but their answer is lacking specific details. The student should have given details on the resolution. The resolution of the light microscope is too low to see the virus. The virus is too small for the resolution of a light microscope, which is within the range 100–300 nm. *This answer is awarded 0 out of 3 marks.*
c The picornavirus binds to receptors on the host cell surface membrane. The membrane folds around the picornavirus forming a sphere which breaks off into the cell.	The student has used the correct scientific words and description for how the virus binds to the host cell surface membrane and the action of the membrane, but has not used the correct word to describe the vesicle (the student used 'sphere' instead of vesicle). The student could also have mentioned the complimentary binding of the virus to the receptors of the host cell in their answer. *This answer is awarded 2 out of 3 marks.*

The following question has an example student response and commentary provided. Work through the question first, then compare your answer to the sample response and commentary. Are your answers different to the sample responses?

2   Fig. 2.1 is a transmission electron micrograph of a cell from the root of the thale cress, *Arabidopsis thaliana*.

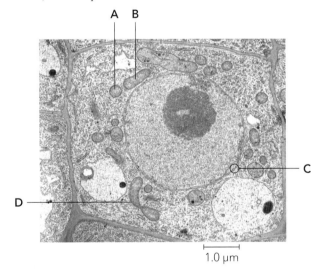

1.0 µm

Fig. 2.1

a   The structures labelled **A** and **B** on Fig. 2.1 are sections of two mitochondria. Suggest why **A** and **B** are different shapes.   [1]

b   Outline the functions of the nucleus in non-dividing cells, such as the cell in Fig. 2.1.   [4]

[Total: 5]

Cambridge International AS & A Level Biology (9700) Paper 21, Q1ai,c, June 2018

Example student response	Commentary
2 **a** The mitochondrion labelled A has been cut through as a cross-section, whereas the mitochondrion labelled B has been cut through as a longitudinal section.	This answer is very well explained. The student could have also said that mitochondria have a variety of shapes or that they are flexible. *This answer is awarded 1 out of 1 mark.*
b The nucleus contains DNA and the DNA base sequence is used in transcription to make mRNA copies of genes.	The answer covers a few key points very concisely. The student could have also discussed the role of the nucleolus in ribosome production. *This answer is awarded 3 out of 4 marks.*

3 Compare your answer to question **2** to the student response and commentary to identify where you could improve your answers. Re-write your answer to any section where you did not score highly. Use the sample answer and commentary to support you.

The following question has an example student response and commentary provided. Work through the question first, then compare your answer to the sample response and commentary. Are your answers different to the sample responses?

4 Starch molecules are the main storage molecules in many types of cereal grain, such as the grain of the barley plant. When the seed inside a barley grain germinates, genes coding for digestive enzymes are switched on. The enzymes that are synthesised catalyse the hydrolysis of storage molecules such as proteins and starch.

a The hydrolysis of proteins in the barley seed produces amino acids that can be used in the synthesis of the proteins required for formation of the seedling (young plant). Fig. 4.1 is an incomplete diagram of the molecular structure of the smallest amino acid, glycine. Each molecule of glycine has two carbon atoms.

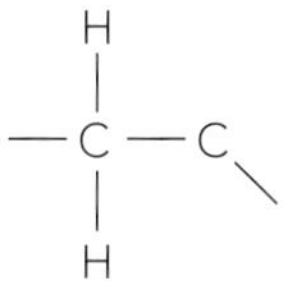

Fig. 4.1

i Complete Fig. 4.1 to show the molecular structure of glycine. [2]

ii Starch is a mixture of two different molecules. Name these **two** molecules. [1]

Two of the enzymes synthesised by the barley seed are α-amylase and maltase. These are involved in the hydrolysis of the stored starch during seedling formation.

In the food industry, the starch extracted from barley seeds (barley starch) is used in the production of sugar syrups. Fig. 4.2 summarises the reactions catalysed by α-amylase in the production of maltose syrup and by maltase in the production of glucose syrup.

$$\text{barley starch} \xrightarrow{\text{α-amylase}} \text{maltose}$$

$$\text{maltose} \xrightarrow{\text{maltase}} \text{glucose}$$

Fig. 4.2

b Some of the substances shown in Fig. 4.2 are listed in Table 4.1.

Complete Table 4.1 to identify which of the terms polysaccharide, monosaccharide and macromolecule apply to each of the substances listed.

Use a tick (✓) if the term applies and a cross (✗) if the term does not apply.

Put a tick (✓) or a cross (✗) in every box.

substance	polysaccharide	monosaccharide	macromolecule
glucose			
maltase			
maltose			
starch			

Table 4.1 [3]

[Total: 6]

Cambridge International AS & A Level Biology (9700) Paper 22, Q2aii,iii,b, March 2021

Example student response	Commentary
4 a i	This student has correctly drawn on the amine group (H₂N) and the remaining part of the carboxylic acid group (C=O and OH). *This answer is awarded 2 out of 2 marks.*
ii amylase and amylopectin	The student has correctly stated amylopectin as one of the molecules starch is made up of. The second molecule starch is made of is amylose. However, the student mistakenly stated amylase, which is an enzyme. *This answer is awarded 0 out of 1 mark.*
b 	substance	polysaccharide	monosaccharide	macromolecule	 glucose: ✗ ✓ ✗ maltase: ✓ ✗ ✓ maltose: ✗ ✗ ✗ starch: ✓ ✗ ✓	The student has correctly completed the rows for glucose, maltose and starch. They gain 1 mark for having both the glucose and starch rows correct, and 1 mark for the maltose row. However, maltase is a protein and not a polysaccharide. Therefore, the row for maltase was incorrect and the final mark is not awarded. *This answer is awarded 2 out of 3 marks.*

Now you have read the commentary to the previous question, here is a question on a similar topic that you should attempt. Use the information from the previous response and commentary to guide you as you answer.

5   Statements **A–E** relate to biological molecules. For each statement, identify the most appropriate term that matches the description.

    A   The molecule formed from a condensation reaction between fructose and glucose.   [1]

    B   The name of the bond broken when two amino acids are separated by hydrolysis.   [1]

    C   The unbranched polymer consisting only of β-glucose molecules.   [1]

    D   The reagent used to test for the presence of proteins.   [1]

    E   The molecule produced, in addition to fatty acids, when a triglyceride is hydrolysed.   [1]

[Total: 5]

Cambridge International AS & A Level Biology (9700) Paper 22, Q1, March 2016

3 Enzymes

KNOWLEDGE FOCUS

In this chapter you will answer questions on:

- what is an enzyme?
- mode of action of enzymes
- investigating the progress of an enzyme-catalysed reaction
- factors that affect enzyme action
- comparing enzyme affinities
- enzyme inhibitors
- immobilising enzymes.

EXAM SKILLS FOCUS

In this chapter you will:

- show that you understand the 'predict' command word and can answer 'predict' questions.

In this chapter, you will practise answering 'predict' questions. Look out for the questions containing this command word and make sure you understand what it means. The definition is given below.

| Predict | suggest what may happen based on available information |

'Predict' questions require you to outline possible outcomes based on data or information given in the question. You may need to combined this with your own knowledge and understanding.

3.1 What is an enzyme?

1   What letters do many enzyme names end in?

2   Contrast an intracellular and extracellular enzyme.   **[Total: 1]**

3.2 Mode of action of enzymes

1   Figure 3.1 shows how an enzyme catalyses the breakdown of a substrate molecule into two product molecules. For each image, write a description of what is happening.

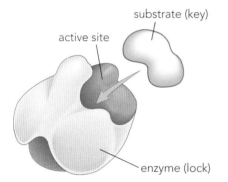 

Picture 1		Picture 2	Picture 3

Figure 3.1: How an enzyme catalyses the breakdown of a substrate molecule

2   There are two hypotheses to explain the action of enzymes.

   a   What are the names of these two hypotheses?

   b   Which is the modern hypothesis, based on more recent evidence that enzyme molecules are more flexible?

3   Define the term 'active site'.   **[Total: 2]**

UNDERSTAND THESE TERMS

- active site
- lock-and-key hypothesis
- induced-fit hypothesis
- activation energy

3.3 Investigating the progress of an enzyme-catalysed reaction

1 If a reaction involves a colour change, what piece of equipment can be used to quantitatively measure this colour change?

2 You can measure the rate of enzyme-catalysed reactions by recording the quantity of product produced over time. Hydrogen peroxide is broken down into water and oxygen by an enzyme. Catalase was added to hydrogen peroxide at time 0. The gas released was collected in a gas syringe, the volume being read at 30 s intervals. Figure 3.2 shows the volume of oxygen produced over time.

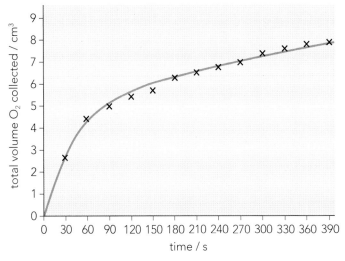

Figure 3.2

    a Explain the curve of the graph between 0 and 390 seconds. [4]

    b Predict the shape of the curve after another 300 seconds and explain your answer. [2]

                                                      [Total: 6]

3 Suggest the advantage of using a colorimeter to determine colour changes, rather than making observations by eye. **[Total: 2]**

> REFLECTION

Were you specific enough in your answer to **2b**? Did you include the reason for your prediction? Make sure you are familiar with the expectation of mark schemes for 'predict' questions.

3.4 Factors that affect enzyme action

1 Copy and complete the table on factors that affect enzyme action.

Factor	What effect the factor has	Why the factor has this effect
temperature		
pH	The rate of reaction decreases either side of the optimum pH.	
enzyme concentration		As the enzyme concentration increases, more enzyme–substrate complexes will form. The rate plateaus when there are more enzymes than substrate present.
	The rate of reaction increases as the substrate concentration increases up until a point, and then the rate plateaus.	As the substrate concentration increases, more enzyme–substrate complexes will form. The rate plateaus as the enzymes become saturated with substrate (all enzyme active sites are in use).

2 What is meant by the term 'V_{max}'?

3 A student carried out an experiment to identify the optimum pH of an enzyme. They carried out the experiment using five different pH buffers and measured the rate of reaction at each pH. Their results are shown in the graph in Figure 3.3.

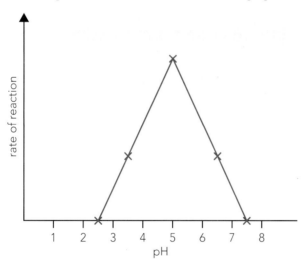

Figure 3.3

Explain why it is not possible to conclude that pH 5 is the optimum pH for this enzyme. **[Total: 2]**

3.5 Comparing enzyme affinities

1   What is the Michaelis–Menten constant (K_m) used for?

2   The enzyme X has a lower affinity for its substrate than enzyme Y.
    Which of the following statements are correct for enzyme X?

    A   X has a higher V_{max} than Y
    B   X has a higher K_m than Y
    C   X has a lower V_{max} than Y
    D   X has a lower K_m than Y   [Total: 1]

≪ RECALL AND CONNECT 2 ≪

Look back at Chapter 2 Biological molecules: State the different bonds in the tertiary structure of a protein.

3.6 Enzyme inhibitors

1   Match up the terms in column A with their definitions in column B.

A	B
Competitive inhibitor	An inhibitor that binds to the enzyme at a site away from the active site, causing a change in shape to the active site.
Non-competitive inhibitor	The inhibitor is not permanently bound to the enzyme.
Reversible inhibition	An inhibitor that is similar in shape to the substrate and that can bind to the active site of the enzyme.

2   Some metabolic reactions are controlled using enzyme inhibitors.
    An example is end-product inhibition, which is when the product of the reaction is a non-competitive reversible inhibitor.

    Suggest why end-product inhibition is important.   [Total: 2]

3   State how the effect on a competitive inhibitor can be reversed.   [Total: 1]

≪ RECALL AND CONNECT 3 ≪

Look back at Chapter 2 Biological molecules: What is a condensation reaction?

UNDERSTAND THESE TERMS

- competitive inhibition
- non-competitive inhibition

3.7 Immobilising enzymes

1 What is an immobilised enzyme?

2 How can sodium alginate solution be used to immobilise enzymes?

3 State and explain two advantages of using immobilised enzymes.   **[Total: 4]**

SELF-ASSESSMENT CHECKLIST

Let's revisit the Knowledge focus and Exam skills focus for this chapter.

Decide how confident you are with each statement.

Now I can:	Show it	Needs more work	Almost there	Confident to move on
state what enzymes are	Add this definition to a key word glossary or flashcard set and test yourself.			
explain the mode of action of enzymes	Draw and annotate a diagram to explain the lock-and-key hypothesis and the induced-fit hypothesis.			
investigate the progress of enzyme-controlled reactions	Describe how measuring the product produced can be used to investigate the progress of an enzyme-controlled reaction.			
outline the use of a colorimeter for measuring the progress of enzyme-catalysed reactions	Describe how a colorimeter could be used to measure the progress of amylase digesting starch, using iodine as an indicator.			
investigate and explain the effect of temperature, pH, enzyme concentration and substrate concentration on the rate of enzyme-catalysed reactions	Answer all the questions in this chapter on how these four variables affect the rate of enzyme-catalysed reactions.			

CONTINUED

Now I can:	Show it	Needs more work	Almost there	Confident to move on
use V_{max} and K_m to compare the affinity of different enzymes for their substrates	Describe how you could use V_{max} and K_m on a graph showing the initial rate of reaction of two enzymes to compare their affinities.			
explain the effects of reversible inhibitors, both competitive and non-competitive, on enzyme activity	Draw and annotate a diagram of an enzyme to indicate where a competitive and a non-competitive inhibitor would bind on to it and the impact that this has on the rate of the reaction it catalyses.			
state the advantages of using immobilised enzymes	Explain one advantage of using immobilised enzymes.			
show that I understand the command word 'predict' and can answer 'predict' questions	Make a list of the key marking points that commonly come up in 'predict' questions for the enzymes topic.			

4 Cell membranes and transport

In this chapter, you will practise answering 'suggest' questions. Look out for the question containing this command word and make sure you understand what it means. The definition is given below.

Suggest	apply knowledge and understanding to situations where there are a range of valid responses in order to make proposals/put forward considerations

The 'suggest' command word can be used in two different ways: sometimes there is no direct answer, other times you need to draw upon your broader knowledge of this subject to answer questions from an unfamiliar context. It is important that you are confident in your understanding and recognise what you should include in your answers.

4.1 The importance of membranes and
4.2 Structure of membranes

1   What are the two functions of the cell surface membrane?

2   State three factors that increase the fluidity of the cell membrane.

3   List the components found in the fluid mosaic model of membrane structure.

4   The fluid-mosaic model of the cell surface membrane is shown in Figure 4.1.

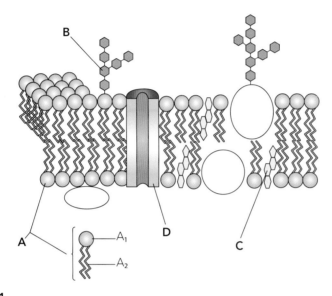

Figure 4.1

a   Identify structures **B**, **C** and **D**.   [3]

b   Structure **A** is a phospholipid. Using Figure 4.1, explain how
     phospholipids are arranged to form the cell surface membrane.   [4]

[Total: 7]

REFLECTION

Dual coding is where your brain processes information in two different pathways
at the same time to strengthen your memory. This is typically used in biology
where you draw annotated diagrams to help visualise models and processes.
How could you use dual coding to learn the arrangements of the molecules in
the cell surface membrane and their functions? Once you have made a diagram,
how could you then use it to build your long-term memory of the content?
Keep in mind that you can improve long-term memory through repeated,
spaced out testing. Can you think of other examples in biology where you
can use dual coding to help you learn and memorise information?

4.3 Roles of the molecules found in membranes

1 What is one function of each of the following components?

   a phospholipids

   b cholesterol

   c glycolipids and glycoproteins

   d proteins

2 What are the key components found in the cell surface membrane?

3 Figure 4.2 shows the structure of a cell surface membrane.

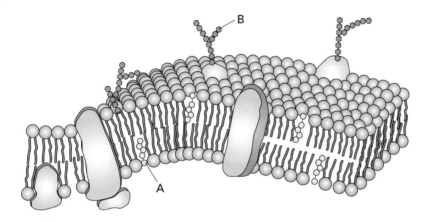

Figure 4.2

   a Explain how the structure of component **A** allows it to do its function.   [4]

   b Explain how the structure of component **B** allows it to do its function.   [3]

                                      [Total: 7]

4 Cell surface membranes are made up of phospholipids.

   a Describe how the phospholipids are arranged to form the cell surface membrane.   [4]

   b Hormones are chemicals that can affect the functioning of organs. They can be classified into peptide hormones or steroid hormones.

      An example of a peptide hormone is insulin, which is a globular protein. It binds onto cell surface receptors to signal cells. Conversely, oestrogen is a steroid hormone, which is made from cholesterol. It can diffuse through the cell surface membrane and cause an effect within the cell directly.

      Using the information given, explain why oestrogen can pass through the cell surface membrane, but insulin cannot.   [4]

                                        [Total: 8]

> **UNDERSTAND THESE TERMS**
>
> - fluid mosaic model
> - glycoprotein
> - cholesterol

Think back to Chapter 2 Biological molecules: How are amino acids in globular proteins arranged? What sort of functions do globular proteins tend to have?

4.4 Cell signalling

1 What are the three main stages in cell signalling?

2 Which statements about ligands may be correct?

I   The secretion of ligands is the second stage of the cell signalling pathway

II   Ligands bind to protein molecules in the cell surface membrane

III Ligands are secreted in response to a stimulus

A   I and II
B   I and III
C   II and III
D   I, II and III

[Total: 1]

« RECALL AND CONNECT 2 «

Think back to Chapter 3: Biological molecules: How does a protein's primary structure determine its overall structure and properties? How does this link to the structure of a transmembrane protein?

UNDERSTAND THESE TERMS

• cell signalling
• ligand

4.5 Movement of substances across membranes

1 Why is it important for cells to be able to carry out diffusion and facilitated diffusion?

2 What is the mechanism that is used in each of the following statements?

a   Root hair cells taking up mineral ions.
b   Sodium ions moving across the membrane down the concentration gradient.
c   White blood cells releasing the digested contents of a pathogen.
d   Water vapour moving out of the stomata.

3 A student investigated how substances **A** and **B** are absorbed into cells in the small intestine.

They placed the cells into solutions with different concentrations of both substances and measured the rate of absorption.

From their calculations, they concluded that substance **A** is absorbed by simple diffusion, whereas substance **B** is absorbed by active transport.

a   Explain the difference between diffusion and active transport.   [4]

b Copy each of the axes in Figure 4.3 and sketch graphs to show how the rate of absorption would change in different concentrations of solutions for substances **A** and **B**. [2]

[Total: 6]

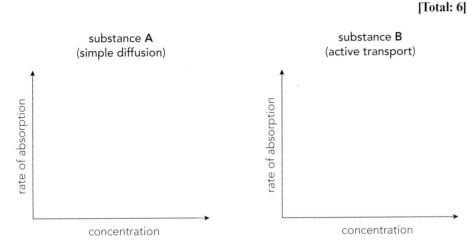

Figure 4.3

4 A student carried out an investigation to estimate the water potential in carrot cells. The following method was used:

- Remove the skin from a carrot. Cut five carrot cylinders from the same carrot using a cork borer.
- Cut them so they have the same length.
- Dry them with a paper towel and measure their mass with a balance. Record their initial mass in a table.
- Place them separately into five boiling tubes with different concentrations of sucrose solutions – 0%, 1%, 2%, 5% and 10%.
- Leave for 24 hours.
- Take the carrot cylinders out from their solutions and blot them dry with some tissue paper.
- Measure their final mass and record it in the table.

a State the dependent and independent variables in this investigation. [2]
b State two variables that were controlled in this investigation. [2]
c Explain how the student should then process the result to determine the change in water potential of the carrot. [4]
d Suggest and explain one improvement to this method to obtain more accurate results. [2]

[Total: 10]

UNDERSTAND THESE TERMS

- water potential
- plasmolysis
- endocytosis
- exocytosis

≪ RECALL AND CONNECT 3 ≪

Think back to Chapter 1 Cell structure: What organelle is responsible for digesting unwanted molecules within the cell? How is this organelle adapted for its function?

REFLECTION

Think of graphic organisers as a way of visually and spatially arranging information to help you organise and memorise it. Research has shown that our spatial awareness has a big impact on how we remember things, such as how you organise your clothes into different drawers in the wardrobe. There are four types of graphic organisers: Chunk; Compare; Sequence; Cause and effect. For example, how could you use a mind map ('chunk') to learn the details and examples of the different transport mechanisms? When you make your own notes in biology, consider what graphic organisers you can use to help you learn and arrange the knowledge. It should allow you to remember facts well and form links between them to help build long-term memory. Think about how the graphic organisers can become a testing tool to help you practise.

SELF-ASSESSMENT CHECKLIST

Let's revisit the Knowledge focus and Exam skills focus for this chapter.

Decide how confident you are with each statement.

Now I can:	Show it	Needs more work	Almost there	Confident to move on
describe the structure of phospholipids and the fluid mosaic model of membrane structure	Draw a diagram of a phospholipid molecule and annotate the different parts of the molecule with their properties.			
describe the arrangement of the molecules in cell surface membranes	Draw a diagram of the fluid mosaic model with labels for each component.			
describe the roles of the molecules found in cell surface membranes	Annotate the diagram of the phospholipid bilayer you drew with the function of each component.			
outline the process of cell signalling	Draw a flowchart to illustrate how one cell can change the function of another cell elsewhere in the body through chemical cell signalling.			
explain how substances enter and leave cells across cell surface membranes	Construct a table to summarise the different transport mechanisms, looking at their definitions, types of molecules they transport, direction of transport and whether they use energy or not.			

CONTINUED				
Now I can:	Show it	Needs more work	Almost there	Confident to move on
carry out practical investigations into diffusion and osmosis	Write a step-by-step method to show how to set up a practical to investigate diffusion and osmosis.			
illustrate the principle that surface area : volume ratios decrease with increasing size	Draw a cube with 1 cm sides and another cube with 2 cm sides. Calculate and compare their surface area : volume ratios.			
explain the movement of water between cells and solutions in terms of water potential	Explain to someone what would happen to an egg if it was placed in pure water compared with if it was placed in concentrated salt solution, using the concept of osmosis and water potential.			
show that I understand the 'suggest' command word and can answer 'suggest' questions	Explain to someone what the command word 'suggest' means and write an example 'suggest' question and mark scheme.			

5 The mitotic cell cycle

In this chapter you will practise answering 'explain' questions. Look out for the questions containing this command word and make sure you understand what it means. The definition is given below.

Explain	say why, give reasons and support your answer with evidence

'Explain' questions usually require a longer response and are worth between 2 and 6 marks. Make sure you plan your answer to make sure all the points you need to include in your answer are covered. Be careful not to write a description instead of an explanation.

An important exam skill is writing to time. The questions in this chapter have different mark allocations. If you check how many marks a question is worth before you answer, you will know roughly how much time to spend and how much detail is required.

5.1 Growth and reproduction

1   What term is given to new cells made by cell division?

2   Suggest how a zygote could grow.

3   Suggest why cell division must be precisely controlled.   **[Total: 1]**

> ## ≪ RECALL AND CONNECT 1 ≪
>
> Think back to Chapter 1 Cell structure: What is the function of the nucleus?

5.2 Chromosomes

1   Draw and label a chromosome made up of two sister chromatids. Include the following structures: telomeres, genes, centromere, sister chromatids.

2   Figure 5.1 shows a set of human chromosomes before cell division occurs.

Explain why each chromosome appears as a double structure.   **[Total: 2]**

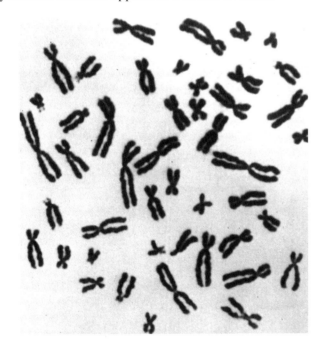

Figure 5.1

5.3 The cell cycle

1   Figure 5.2 is a diagram representing the cell cycle.
    State the names of the stages of the cell cycle represented as **A**, **B**, **C** and **D**.

UNDERSTAND THESE TERMS
• chromatid
• mitosis
• cell cycle

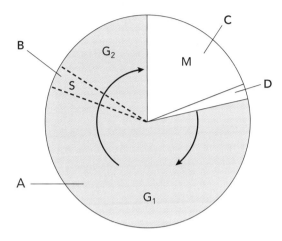

Figure 5.2: The mitotic cell cycle

2   Match each stage of interphase to the correct description.

Stage of interphase	Description
G_1	DNA in the nucleus replicates.
S	RNA, enzymes and proteins for growth are created.
G_2	The cell grows and the replicated DNA is checked for copying errors.

3   State which stage of the cell cycle follows interphase.   **[Total: 1]**

5.4 Mitosis

1 Why is mitosis important?

2 Figure 5.3 shows two animal cells undergoing mitosis.
Identify which stage of mitosis the cells are currently in. **[Total: 1]**

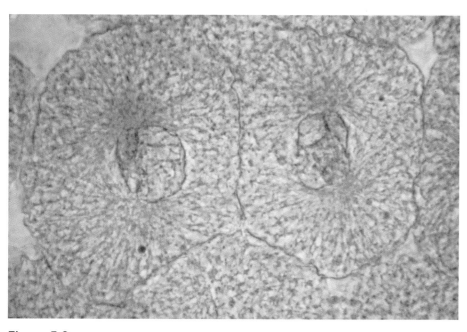

Figure 5.3

3 Describe the behaviour of the cell during metaphase. **[Total: 3]**

≪ RECALL AND CONNECT 2 ≪

Look back at Chapter 1 Cell structure: What is the nuclear envelope?

REFLECTION

How long did you spend answering question **3**? You will find you become quicker at answering exam questions as you become more experienced and can recall the information more readily, but you can also improve your speed by making sure the number of statements you include matches the number of marks. This should help you to be more concise and therefore quicker.

5.5 The role of telomeres

1 Some scientists have suggested that if we could prevent the loss of telomeres we could slow down or prevent ageing. Suggest why this would prevent ageing.

2 Describe the function of the telomeres. **[Total: 2]**

UNDERSTAND THESE TERMS
- telomere
- stem cell

5.6 The role of stem cells

1 What is a stem cell?

2 Describe how stem cells can replace cells in tissues. **[Total: 2]**

5.7 Cancers

1 What is a mutation, and how can this result in tumour growth?

2 Give the name for when cancer cells break off and spread to another organ. **[Total: 1]**

UNDERSTAND THESE TERMS
- tumour
- mutation
- carcinogen

SELF-ASSESSMENT CHECKLIST

Let's revisit the Knowledge focus and Exam skills focus for this chapter.

Decide how confident you are with each statement.

Now I can:	Show it	Needs more work	Almost there	Confident to move on
describe the structure of chromosomes	Draw and label a chromosome.			
outline the cell cycle – the cycle of events by which body cells grow to a certain size and then divide into two	List the stages of the cell cycle in order and describe what happens at each stage.			
describe the behaviour of chromosomes during mitosis and the associated behaviour of the nuclear envelope, the cell surface membrane and the spindle	Describe what happens during prophase, metaphase, anaphase and telophase and focus on the position and movement of the chromosomes.			
identify stages of mitosis in photomicrographs, diagrams and microscope slides	Search for mitosis photomicrographs online and identify which stage of mitosis the cells are in.			

CONTINUED

Now I can:	Show it	Needs more work	Almost there	Confident to move on
explain the importance of mitosis	Write a paragraph to explain the importance of mitosis.			
outline the role of telomeres	Describe the role of telomeres.			
outline the role of stem cells	Describe the role of stem cells.			
explain how uncontrolled cell division can lead to cancer	Write a paragraph explaining how uncontrolled cell division can lead to tumour growth.			
show that I understand the command word 'explain' and can answer 'explain' questions	Explain to someone what the command word 'explain' means and write an example question and mark scheme.			

Exam practice 2

This section contains past paper questions from previous Cambridge exams, which draw together your knowledge on a range of topics that you have covered up to this point. These questions give you the opportunity to test your knowledge and understanding. Additional past paper practice questions can be found in the accompanying digital material.

The following question has an example student response and commentary provided. Work through the question first, then compare your answer to the sample response and commentary. Are your answers different to the sample responses?

1   Trypsin is a protease enzyme found in the digestive system. Fig. 1.1 shows how the substrate concentration affects the rate of reaction of trypsin.

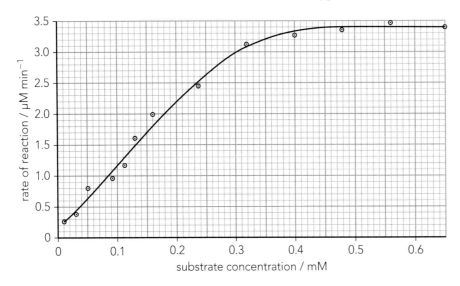

Fig. 1.1

a   Use Fig. 1.1 to:

   i   determine V_{max} for trypsin.   [1]

   ii   calculate K_m for trypsin. Show your working.   [2]

b   Describe **and** explain the shape of the curve in Fig. 1.1.   [4]

c   Trypsin is composed of one polypeptide chain of 223 amino acids. The active site of trypsin contains three amino acids which catalyse a hydrolysis reaction. These three amino acids occupy the following positions in the primary structure of trypsin:

   •   histidine, position 57

   •   aspartate, position 102

   •   serine, position 195.

    i   In the functioning enzyme, these three amino acids are close together in the active site. Explain how the structure of the protein makes this possible. [3]

    ii   When trypsin acts on a substrate, another substance is required as a reactant. Name this other substance. [1]

[Total: 11]

Cambridge International AS & A Level Biology (9700) Paper 23, Q2, June 2016

Example student response	Commentary
1 a i 3.4	The student has correctly determined V_{max}, by reading off the rate of reaction at the maximum rate of reaction on the graph. However, no mark is awarded as they did not include the units. 3.4 µM min^{-1} is the full answer. *This answer is awarded 0 out of 1 mark.*
ii $\dfrac{3.4}{2} = 1.7$	This answer shows that the student has correctly calculated ½V_{max}, which would gain them 1 mark. However, they have not then drawn a line from here to the line of best fit, and then down to the x-axis to work out the substrate concentration, which is the K_m. The answer was 0.15 mM. *This answer is awarded 1 out of 2 marks.*
b At the low substrate concentration, there is a directly proportional relationship up to 0.25 mM. At the higher substrate concentrations, there is a less steep increase in the rate.	The student has given three valid descriptions in this answer, but they have not addressed the second command word 'explain'. For this question, you could gain a maximum of 3 marks if you only gave descriptions, as the question asked you to describe and explain. To improve this answer, the student could have explained that at 0.45 mM the rate levelled off because all the active sites were occupied. *This answer is awarded 3 out of 4 marks.*

2   Now compare your answers to question **1** to the commentary to identify how you could improve your answers.

The following question has an example student response and commentary provided. Work through the question first, then compare your answer to the sample response and commentary. Are your answers different to the sample responses?

3   T-helper lymphocytes and Leydig cells are two types of mammalian cells. The main role of T-helper lymphocytes and Leydig cells is to synthesise and secrete cell-signalling molecules.

- T-helper lymphocytes synthesise proteins known as cytokines.

- Leydig cells synthesise the steroid (lipid) hormone testosterone from cholesterol.

- Leydig cells also synthesise cholesterol.

a   State **one** way in which cytokines are involved in an immune response.   [1]

b   Fig. 3.1 shows part of a mammalian cell.

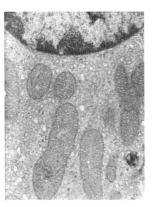

Fig. 3.1

   i   State, with reasons, whether Fig. 3.1 shows part of a Leydig cell or part of a T-helper lymphocyte.   [2]

   ii   Underline the correct name for the type of image shown in Fig. 3.1 and explain your choice.   [2]

     •   photomicrograph

     •   scanning electron micrograph

     •   transmission electron micrograph.

c   Testosterone molecules and cytokine molecules are transported in the circulatory system to reach their target cells. Testosterone molecules are able to enter their target cells and bind to receptors within the cytoplasm.

   i   Outline one way in which testosterone molecules could enter their target cells.   [2]

   ii   Cytokine molecules are not able to enter their target cells. Suggest and explain why cytokine molecules are not able to cross the cell surface membrane to enter their target cells.   [2]

[Total: 9]

Cambridge International AS & A Level Biology (9700) Paper 22, Q3, March 2021

Example student response	Commentary
3 **a** Cytokines are used to attract more phagocytes to the infection site.	The answer is correct in describing an effect of cytokines in an immune response. *This answer is awarded 1 out of 1 mark.*
b **i** It is a Leydig cell since the image does not show any ribosomes or rough endoplasmic reticulum.	While this answer correctly describes the image, it did not explain how the absence of ribosomes and rough ER links to the functions of the Leydig cell, which is the crucial determining factor. It is because the Leydig cell produces mainly lipids and not proteins, therefore you would not expect it to have many or any ribosomes or rough ER. *This answer is awarded 1 out of 2 marks.*

Example student response	Commentary
ii Transmission electron micrograph Explanation: It shows a 2D image and not a 3D image, so it must be taken with a transmission electron microscope that only produces 2D images.	The student should follow the instructions carefully to underline their choice, although this will not deduct points as the answer itself is correct. However, the explanation is not exclusive to the TEM as photomicrographs also can only be in 2D. The unique point about TEM is that they produce 2D images with the cell ultrastructure shown in detail – this is different from photomicrographs that do not show the cell ultrastructure, and also from scanning electron micrographs that show the 3D surface of cells instead of the inner structure in a thin layer. *This answer is awarded 1 out of 2 marks.*
c i Testosterone can enter its target cells by diffusion because it is a lipid molecule and can pass through the fatty acid core.	This is a good answer as it clearly states the transport mechanism and gives a concise explanation with the key detail on why it can do that. *This answer is awarded 2 out of 2 marks.*
ii Cytokine is a protein which means it is hydrophilic. This means it cannot cross the cell surface membrane to enter the target cell.	This answer shows that the student has read the question about cytokines being proteins and has an idea about the hydrophilic and hydrophobic properties. However, their understanding was not made clear and they repeated part of the question instead of explicitly stating how hydrophilic substances cannot pass through the hydrophobic core of the phospholipid bilayer. *This answer is awarded 1 out of 2 marks.*

Now you have read the commentary to the previous question, here is a similar question that you should attempt. Use the information from the previous response and commentary to guide you as you answer.

4 *Hakea* spp. are xerophytic plants native to Australia. The leaves of *Hakea* have adaptations for a xerophytic mode of life.

When the availability of phosphate ions and other soil nutrients is limited, a number of changes occur in the roots of *Hakea* spp.:

- Regions of meristematic tissue are active for a few days.

- Root clusters are formed. A root cluster is a dense arrangement of tiny side roots known as rootlets.

- Most of the epidermal cells of the rootlets are root hair cells.

- Rootlets release compounds into the soil that make phosphates and other mineral ions more soluble for uptake.

- Uptake of phosphate ions and the absorption of water from the soil increases.

a   Organic anions (negatively charged organic compounds) are released into the soil by rootlets. The concentration of these organic anions can become higher in the soil solution than in the rootlet cells.

Suggest **and** explain how the concentration of organic anions in the soil solution can become higher than in the rootlet cells.   [3]

b   Explain how the formation of root clusters can lead to an increase in the uptake of phosphate ions and absorption of water from the soil solution.   [2]

[Total: 5]

Cambridge International AS & A Level Biology (9700) Paper 23, Q3bii,iii, June 2022

The following question has an example student response and commentary provided. Work through the question first, then compare your answer to the sample response and commentary. Are your answers different to the sample responses?

5   Fig. 5.1 shows a stage in the mitotic cell cycle in an animal cell.

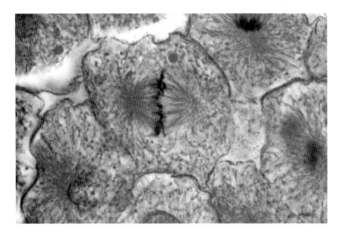

Fig. 5.1

a   i   Name the stage of mitosis shown in Fig. 5.1.   [1]

ii   State **three** features which are characteristic of the stage of mitosis shown in Fig. 5.1.   [3]

b   Explain the importance of mitosis in organisms.   [3]

c   In many multicellular organisms, such as mammals, the time taken for the mitotic cell cycle varies considerably between different tissues, but is very carefully controlled in each cell. Suggest the importance of this control in mammals.   [2]

[Total: 9]

Cambridge International AS & A Level Biology (9700) Paper 23, Q1, June 2011

Example student response	Commentary
5 a i Metaphase	The student correctly identified this stage as metaphase. *This answer is awarded 1 out of 1 mark.*
ii • The chromosomes are lined up at the equator of the cell. • There are spindle fibres present. • The spindle is released from centrioles.	Their first point was correct and in sufficient detail. Their second point was lacking important details. The student should also have included what the spindle fibres are attached to and where the centrioles are located. Lastly, they should have said that the spindle fibres are attached to the centromeres. *This answer is awarded 1 out of 3 marks.*
b Mitosis is very important to make new cells to replace damaged tissues or for growth.	The student has correctly identified the fundamental importance of mitosis in a very concise way. The student scored 1 mark for saying that mitosis replaces cells, specifying that it replaces damaged tissues and finally for saying it is used for growth. *This answer is awarded 3 out of 3 marks.*
c The control is important to co-ordinate growth in the mammal.	The student has not given enough detail in their response. Although the sentence is correct, the student should also include the importance of minimising alterations to DNA during cell division to prevent tumour formation. *This answer is awarded 1 out of 2 marks.*

6   Compare your answer to question **5** to the student response and commentary to identify where you could improve your answers. Re-write your answer to any section where you did not score highly. Use the sample answer and commentary to support you.

6 Nucleic acids and protein synthesis

6.1 The molecule of life and
6.2 The structure of DNA and RNA

1   State two features that are essential for a molecule that carries genetic information.

2   Draw and label: a DNA nucleotide, an RNA nucleotide and an ATP molecule.

≪ RECALL AND CONNECT 1 ≪

Think back to Chapter 1 Cell structure: Name all the organelles in a plant cell that contain DNA.

---

3   The table shows some of the percentage of bases present in one human gene.
Use these data to calculate the percentage of adenine and thymine bases present.

% adenine	% guanine	% thymine	% cytosine
26.4	23.6		

[Total: 1]

4   Compare the similarities and differences between a DNA nucleotide
and an RNA nucleotide.   [Total: 3]

REFLECTION

Did you manage to gain 3 marks for the 'compare' question? One common error in this question is that students miss that the question says 'nucleotide' and they compare the polymers instead. If you made this mistake, try highlighting important instructions within exam questions.

6.3 DNA replication

1   DNA polymerase and DNA ligase are two enzymes involved in DNA replication.

Match each enzyme to its function.

Enzyme	Function
DNA polymerase	An enzyme that catalyses the joining together of two nucleotides with covalent phosphodiester bonds during DNA replication.
DNA ligase	An enzyme that copies DNA; it runs along the separated DNA strands lining up one complementary nucleotide at a time ready for joining by DNA ligase.

2 Figure 6.1 shows a section of DNA being replicated, demonstrating the formation of the leading and lagging strands of the replicated DNA.

What is meant by the leading and lagging strands?

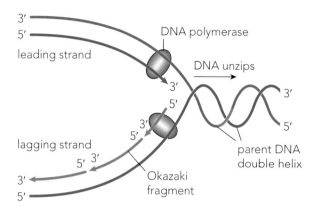

Figure 6.1: Diagram of DNA replication

3 The method of copying DNA is described as being 'semi-conservative'. Explain what this term means. **[Total: 2]**

REFLECTION

Were you clear enough in this answer? The mark scheme specifies that you must state one strand is new, and not just 50% is new. Just stating 50% could mean a mixture of each strand is new. To help you remember this, try making a flashcard with this definition and highlight the word 'strand'.

UNDERSTAND THESE TERMS

- nucleotide
- dinucleotide
- polynucleotide
- phosphodiester bond

6.4 The genetic code

1 There are 20 different amino acids and four different bases. A triplet of bases codes for one amino acid.

How many different triplet combinations of bases exist?

≪ RECALL AND CONNECT 2 ≪

Think back to Chapter 2 Biological molecules: What is the primary structure of a protein?

UNDERSTAND THESE TERMS

- complementary base pairing
- DNA polymerase
- DNA ligase

2 State the name of the

a strand of a DNA molecule that is used in transcription [1]

b second strand of a DNA molecule. [1]

[Total: 2]

6.5 Protein synthesis

1 Draw and annotate a diagram to demonstrate the process of:

   a transcription

   b translation

2 After transcription, the primary transcript is modified (RNA processing).
Describe RNA processing. **[Total: 2]**

3 Describe the process of transcription. **[Total: 5]**

6.6 Gene mutations

1 The original DNA base sequence of a section of one gene is:

AGC|CCT|GAT|GGC|CCA

a–c show three gene mutations that have occurred to this original strand.
What type of gene mutation has occurred in **a**, **b** and **c** to cause these alterations
to the original strand?

   a AGC|CCT|GAT|GGC|CA

   b AGC|CCT|GTT|GGC|CCA

   c AGC|CCT|GAT|AGG|CCC|A

2 Suggest why a substitution mutation may not result in a different
amino acid being coded for. **[Total: 2]**

SELF-ASSESSMENT CHECKLIST

Let's revisit the Knowledge focus and Exam skills focus for this chapter.

Decide how confident you are with each statement.

Now I can:	Show it	Needs more work	Almost there	Confident to move on
describe the structure of nucleotides, including ATP	Draw and label DNA, RNA and ATP.			
describe briefly the structures of the bases found in DNA and RNA (adenine, guanine, thymine, cytosine and uracil)	For each base, state whether it is a purine or pyrimidine.			
describe the structure of DNA	Draw a diagram of the DNA polymer and double helix and annotate the structure.			

CONTINUED

Now I can:	Show it	Needs more work	Almost there	Confident to move on
describe the structure of RNA, using messenger RNA as an example	Write a paragraph describing the structure of mRNA.			
describe the semi-conservative replication of DNA	Create a flow diagram outlining the stages that occur in DNA replication.			
explain how the sequence of amino acids in a polypeptide is coded for by a sequence of nucleotides in DNA (a gene)	Describe the process of transcription and translation.			
describe the principle of the universal genetic code in which DNA bases code for amino acids plus start and stop signals	Write a paragraph describing what is meant by the term 'universal' when describing the genetic code.			
compare and contrast the roles of DNA and RNA in the transcription and translation stages of protein synthesis	Draw a diagram demonstrating transcription and translation. Annotate the diagram to describe the role of DNA and RNA at each point they appear in the diagram. You can also use a comparison table to summarise your information.			
explain the modification of RNA after transcription and the nature of introns and exons	Draw a labelled diagram of mRNA before and after the post-transcriptional modifications.			
compare and contrast the nature, types and effects of gene mutations	List the types of gene mutations that occur and explain the effect each can have.			
show that I understand connections between concepts	Create a concept map demonstrating links between the theories within this topic. You could draw lines between each concept and write the connection between the theories on each line.			

7 Transport in plants

KNOWLEDGE FOCUS

In this chapter you will answer questions on:

- the transport needs of plants
- the vascular system: xylem and phloem
- the structure of stems, roots and leaves and the distribution of xylem and phloem
- the transport of water
- the transport of assimilates.

EXAM SKILLS FOCUS

In this chapter you will:

- show that you understand the command word 'state' and can answer 'state' questions.

Questions often ask you for a fact or short answer. For example, in this topic you may be asked to provide the names of different structures of stems, roots or leaves. The 'state' command word is often used for short-answer questions. The definition for 'state' is shown below.

| State | express in clear terms |

Do not provide too much information or detail when you answer 'state' questions – they are often only worth one mark. However, 'state' is sometimes combined with another word, such as 'explain' or 'suggest' and will be worth more than one mark; so remember to answer both parts.

7.1 The transport needs of plants

1   Which substances do the roots absorb?

2   Sugars, such as glucose, are produced in the leaves by photosynthesis.
All the cells of the plant require a supply of glucose.

    a   Give the name of the process that glucose is required for in all cells.   [1]

    b   Describe the role of glucose in making the cell wall.   [3]

[Total: 4]

≪ RECALL AND CONNECT 1 ≪

Think back to Chapter 4 Cell membranes and transport: What is the role of cholesterol in the cell surface membrane?

7.2 Vascular system: xylem and phloem

1   Xylem and phloem tissues make up the two vascular systems in plants.
For each statement, indicate whether it describes the role of xylem or phloem.

    a   carries water and inorganic ions

    b   carries organic substances made in photosynthesis

    c   transports substances from the leaves to other parts of the plant

    d   transports water from the roots in one direction.

> **UNDERSTAND THESE TERMS**
> - vascular system
> - vascular
> - vascular tissue

2   Give two differences between the vascular systems in plants
and mammals.   **[Total: 2]**

3   State the name of the fluid inside xylem vessels and explain how
the xylem wall is adapted to transport this fluid.   **[Total: 3]**

REFLECTION

Did you manage to get three marks for question **3** in this section? Did you remember to include answers for both command words in the question? For three-mark questions such as these, always check your answer to make sure you have included what you consider to be three different marking points. You may find it helpful to underline what you think is the key term or phrase to visually make it easier to check.

7.3 Structure of stems, roots and leaves and the distribution of xylem and phloem

1   Copy and complete the paragraph below using appropriate terms.

In stems and veins of leaves, the xylem and .... are found in structures called .... , which also contain other types of cells. In roots, the xylem and phloem are found at the .... of the root.

2   What is the name for the cap of fibres on the vascular bundle and what is its function?

3   Sketch a low-power diagram of the young buttercup stem's transverse section (TS) shown in Figure 7.1.   **[Total: 4]**

UNDERSTAND THESE TERMS

- parenchyma
- collenchyma
- dicotyledon
- epidermis
- endodermis

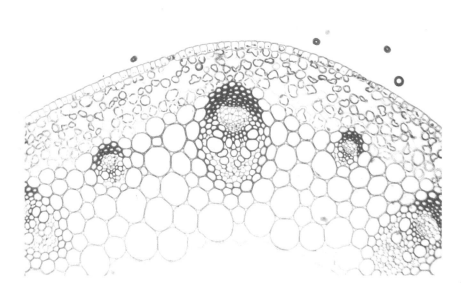

Figure 7.1

7.4 The transport of water

1   Xerophytes are plants adapted to live in environments with limited water. How are their leaves adapted to survive in these conditions?

2   Once water has been absorbed from the soil into the root hair cells by osmosis, it must travel to the xylem to be transported to the rest of the plant. This occurs by either the apoplast or symplast pathway.

Describe the differences between the apoplast and symplast pathways.   **[Total: 3]**

3   Explain the role of the Casparian strip in the movement of water from the root hair cells to the xylem.   **[Total: 3]**

UNDERSTAND THESE TERMS

- stoma
- mesophyll
- transpiration
- cuticle
- xylem vessel

<< RECALL AND CONNECT 2 <<

Think back to Chapter 4 Cell membranes and transport: What are the five basic mechanisms by which exchange across a membrane occurs?

7.5 Transport of assimilates

1   What creates the pressure difference in the phloem to cause the mass flow of phloem sap?

2   Assimilates are transported from sources to sinks. What are examples of sinks?

3   Describe how the structure of a sieve tube element differs from the structure of a companion cell.   **[Total: 4]**

UNDERSTAND THESE TERMS

- sieve tube element
- companion cell
- sieve tube

SELF-ASSESSMENT CHECKLIST

Let's revisit the Knowledge focus and Exam skills focus for this chapter.

Decide how confident you are with each statement.

Now I can:	Show it	Needs more work	Almost there	Confident to move on
outline the transport needs of plants and the fact that some mineral ions and organic compounds can be transported within plants dissolved in water	List the reasons why plants need water, mineral ions and organic compounds.			
draw, label and describe the overall structure of herbaceous dicotyledonous stems, roots and leaves using a light microscope	Search online for a micrograph of a dicotyledonous root. Draw, label and annotate a low-power diagram of this image.			
draw the structure of the transport tissues xylem and phloem using the high-power lens of a light microscope	Search online for a micrograph of xylem and phloem tissues. Draw and label a high-power diagram of these images.			
explain the process of transpiration	Create a flow diagram of the stages of transpiration.			
describe the adaptations of the leaves of xerophytic plants with the aid of annotated drawings	Draw and label the structure of a xerophytic leaf and annotate each structure to explain the adaptation.			

Now I can:	Show it	Needs more work	Almost there	Confident to move on
explain how water moves across a leaf through the apoplast and symplast pathways	Write a paragraph to explain how water moves through both the apoplast and symplast pathways.			
relate the structure of xylem to its functions	Create a flashcard for each structural feature of the xylem and on the reverse of the card describe how the structure relates to the function.			
explain the movement of water up the xylem from root to leaf, including the roles of cohesion–tension and adhesion	Write a paragraph to explain how water moves up the xylem.			
describe the transport of water from the soil to the root xylem through the apoplast and symplast pathways	Write a bullet point list of the route water takes from the root hair cell to the xylem for both the apoplast and symplast pathways.			
relate the structure of phloem to its functions	Create a flashcard for each structural feature of the phloem and on the reverse of the card describe how the structure relates to the function.			
explain that assimilates dissolved in water, such as sucrose and amino acids, move through phloem sieve tubes from sources to sinks	Draw a flow diagram with explanations of how the assimilate moves from sources to sinks in phloem.			
explain mass flow in phloem sieve tubes down a hydrostatic pressure gradient from source to sink	Draw and annotate a diagram of phloem to explain how mass flow occurs.			
explain how companion cells transfer assimilates to phloem sieve tubes	Write an explanation of the role of a companion cell.			
show that I understand the 'state' command word and can answer 'state' questions	Write a simple set of flashcards for this topic, with simple 'state' questions on one side, and their short succinct answers on the other side.			

8 Transport in mammals

Part of the challenge of exams is making sure you do not run out of time. In order to achieve this, make sure you spend an appropriate amount of time on each question. In this chapter, try to answer the questions in timed conditions. The Exam skills chapter provides more support and strategies for answering questions under timed conditions.

8.1 Transport systems in animals and 8.2 The mammalian circulatory system

1 Why do animals require more energy to survive than plants do?

2 'Transport systems are important in large animals to make sure that enough gases reach all cells for respiration. Respiration requires a good supply of oxygen.'

Suggest how this statement could be improved.

≪ RECALL AND CONNECT 1 ≪

Think back to Chapter 6 Nucleic acids and protein synthesis: What determines the sequence of the amino acid chain, which determines the 3D structure shape of proteins such as haemoglobin?

3 Figure 8.1 is a diagram of the mammalian closed double circulatory system. Label the diagram to show: the heart, the lungs, the systemic circulation and the pulmonary circulation.

Figure 8.1: The mammalian closed double circulatory system

4 Describe the function of the pulmonary artery and pulmonary vein. **[Total: 2]**

5 Humans have a double circulatory system. Suggest the advantage to humans of having a double circulatory system. **[Total: 4]**

REFLECTION

Do you know how long it took you to answer the two exam skills questions in this section? Try to answer the remaining exam skills questions in this chapter in timed conditions to monitor how long it takes you. One way to help you speed up is to bullet point your answers.

8.3 Blood vessels

1   Copy and complete the table.

Property	Arteries	Veins
Muscle layer	Thick, so that constriction and dilation can occur to control the volume of blood.	
Elastic layer		Relatively thin as the pressure is much lower.
Wall thickness	Thick, to help prevent the vessels from bursting due to the high pressure.	Thin as the pressure is much lower so there is a low risk of bursting. The thinness means the vessels are easily flattened, which helps the flow of blood up to the heart.
Valves		

UNDERSTAND THESE TERMS

- artery
- vein
- arteriole
- venule

2   The blood in the veins is at a low pressure. Despite this low pressure, the blood is still able to be returned to the heart from your feet, even when stood up. How is this possible?

3   When blood moves from the ventricles into the aorta and pulmonary artery, the blood pressure fluctuates. Explain what causes the fluctuations in pressure in these arteries.   [Total: 2]

8.4 Tissue fluid

1   What is the main component of tissue fluid?

2   Describe how tissue fluid is formed.   [Total: 2]

3   State two functions of tissue fluid.   [Total: 2]

8.5 Blood

1   The behaviour of haemoglobin can be represented on a haemoglobin dissociation curve. Why is the curve S-shaped?

2   Where in the human body would you expect haemoglobin to be most saturated with oxygen?

3   Contrast the structure and function of a red and a white blood cell.   **[Total: 6]**

« RECALL AND CONNECT 2 «

Think back to Chapter 5 The mitotic cell cycle: Lymphocytes are able to detect non-self cells. What type of non-self cells can form when the cell cycle occurs uncontrollably?

UNDERSTAND THESE TERMS

- neutrophil
- monocyte
- macrophage
- lymphocyte

8.6 The heart

1   State the stages of the cardiac cycle.

2   There is a delay between when the atria and the ventricles contract. Explain what causes the delay.   **[Total: 3]**

3   State the role of the coronary arteries.   **[Total: 1]**

SELF-ASSESSMENT CHECKLIST

Let's revisit the Knowledge focus and Exam skills focus for this chapter.

Decide how confident you are with each statement.

Now I can:	Show it	Needs more work	Almost there	Confident to move on
describe the structure of the mammalian circulatory system	Draw and label a diagram of the mammalian circulatory system.			
explain how the structures of arteries, veins and capillaries are related to their functions	Sketch each blood vessel. Describe the structure of each and say how the structural features relate to the function.			
describe and explain the structure and functions of blood, including the transport of oxygen and carbon dioxide	Write a paragraph to describe the structure of each blood cell and the composition of plasma. Explain how each structural feature helps with the function.			

CONTINUED

Now I can:	Show it	Needs more work	Almost there	Confident to move on
make diagrams of blood vessels and blood cells from slides, photomicrographs or electron micrographs	Search online for micrographs of each blood vessel. Draw a scientific diagram of each.			
describe the formation and functions of tissue fluid	Create a flow diagram outlining the stages of how tissue fluid is formed.			
explain the structure and function of the heart	Source or draw a labelled diagram of the heart. Annotate your diagram with the function of each labelled feature.			
describe the cardiac cycle and its control	Write out the stages of the cardiac cycle in a circle. On the lines connecting each stage of the cycle, write an explanation of what causes that stage to occur.			
manage the distribution of my time	Answer three long answer questions in a row in timed conditions.			

Exam practice 3

This section contains past paper questions from previous Cambridge exams, which draw together your knowledge on a range of topics that you have covered up to this point. These questions give you the opportunity to test your knowledge and understanding. Additional past paper practice questions can be found in the accompanying digital material.

The following question has an example student response and commentary provided. Work through the question first, then compare your answer to the sample response and commentary. Are your answers different to the sample responses?

1 **a** Fig. 1.1 is a diagram of a monomer of the nucleic acid, messenger RNA.

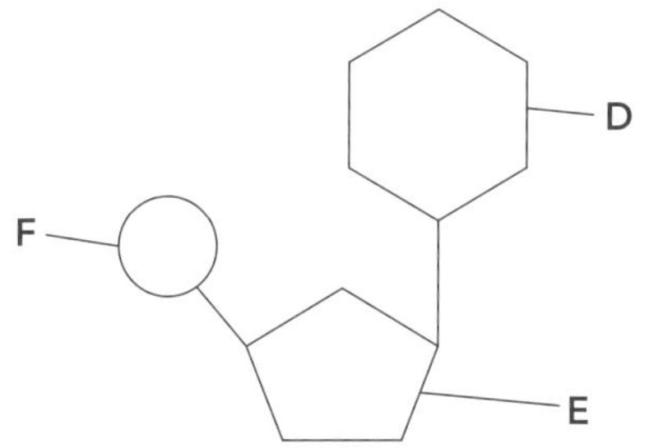

Fig. 1.1

    i Name **D**, **E** and **F** in Fig. 1.1. [3]

    ii State **one** way in which the structure of DNA differs from the structure of messenger RNA. [1]

b Telomeres are repeating sequences of bases located at the ends of DNA molecules. These repeating sequences do not code for proteins.

    The enzyme telomerase ensures that telomeres do not shorten each time DNA is replicated.

    Fig. 1.2A shows the end of a DNA molecule during replication. DNA polymerase cannot attach to the region labelled **X**, so it cannot complete the synthesis of the new strand without the action of telomerase.

Fig. 1.2A

Telomerase synthesises additional lengths of DNA that are added to the telomere. These additional lengths are used by DNA polymerase to complete the process of replication.

Fig. 1.2B is an enlarged view of region **X** to show the action of the enzyme telomerase.

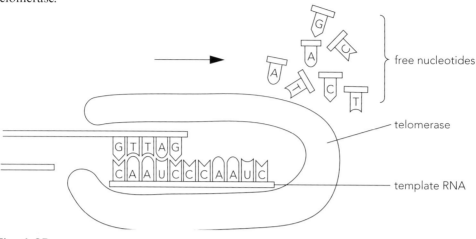

free nucleotides

telomerase

template RNA

Fig. 1.2B

Telomerase contains a short length of RNA that acts as a template for the synthesis of DNA as shown in Fig. 1.2B. Explain how a molecule of telomerase synthesises additional lengths of DNA. [4]

[Total: 8]

Cambridge International AS & A Level Biology (9700) Paper 23, Q3, November 2018

Example student response	Commentary

1 a i   D = base
 	
     E = pentose
 	
     F = phosphate
	The student correctly named structures D and F. While E is a pentose sugar, this is insufficient detail. The question states the molecule is mRNA, and therefore the student would have to specify that the pentose sugar is ribose.
	This answer is awarded 2 out of 3 marks.

ii DNA is made up of two polynucleotide chains, whereas mRNA is made up of one polynucleotide chain.	This is a correct comparison. Other accepted comparisons include: • DNA contains deoxyribose, whereas mRNA contains ribose. • DNA can have the base thymine, whereas mRNA has uracil instead of thymine. • DNA has base pairs due to it being double-stranded, whereas mRNA does not. • DNA forms a helix, whereas mRNA is straight. • DNA is longer than mRNA. *This answer is awarded 1 out of 1 mark.*
b The RNA template will attach to the part labelled X. Free-floating DNA nucleotides will align with the RNA. Bonds form between the DNA nucleotides to form the new chain.	The student correctly described that the RNA template would bind to the part labelled X, but didn't state what that is, so only gains 1 mark, for their first paragraph. Their second paragraph would only score 1 mark, for mentioning the DNA nucleotides aligning with RNA. The student also needs to specify the type of bonds that form. *This answer is awarded 2 out of 4 marks.*

2   Now compare your answers to question **1** to the commentary to identify how you
    could improve your answers.

The following question has an example student response and commentary provided.
Work through the question first, then compare your answer to the sample response and
commentary. Are your answers different to the sample responses? Are there any areas
in which you feel you need to improve your understanding?

3 **a** With reference to the structure of a leaf, explain the difference between
        evaporation and transpiration.   [4]

    b Apple, *Pyrus malus*, sour cherry, *Prunus cerasus*, and peach, *Prunus
        persica*, are dicotyledonous trees that are of importance to commercial
        growers for the fruit that they produce.

        A student chose a small area of land where all three species of fruit tree were
        growing. Leaf samples were removed and, using a microscope, the mean
        number of stomata per square millimetre was estimated for each species.

        The rate of transpiration of each species was then measured on each of three
        separate occasions. The student performed the investigation outside where
        the trees were located and recorded the weather conditions on each day.

        The mean transpiration rate was calculated per unit area of leaf.

        The results are shown in Table 3.1.

fruit tree	mean number of stomata / mm^{-2}	mean transpiration rate / $cm^3\ h^{-1}$		
		hot dry day	warm dry day	warm rainy day
apple	266	0.19	0.35	0.21
sour cherry	284	0.09	0.28	0.25
peach	190	0.03	0.08	0.07

Table 3.1

    i   With reference to Table 3.1, describe and explain the results of
            the investigation.   [3]

    ii The mean transpiration rate of each species was calculated over
            a 24 hour period.

            Describe how the transpiration rate during the night would differ
            from the transpiration rate during the day.

            Explain your answer.   [3]

                                                                      [Total: 10]

Cambridge International AS & A Level Biology (9700) Paper 22, Q3, June 2012

Example student response	Commentary
3 a Evaporation is when liquid water is converted into water vapour, whereas transpiration is the loss of water vapour through the stomata.	The student has given an accurate definition of what evaporation and transpiration are. Each of these definitions gained them 1 mark. To gain the additional 2 marks, they needed to also compare what causes each process to occur. Evaporation requires heat energy to convert the liquid water into its gaseous state, whereas water vapour leaves the stomata due to diffusion down a water potential gradient. *This answer is awarded 2 out of 4 marks.*
b i The mean rate of transpiration is lowest on the hot dry day, for sour cherry the rate is 0.09 but on a warm dry day it is 0.28 and a warm rainy day it is 0.25. The peach has the lowest mean number of stomata and the rate of transpiration is lowest for this fruit tree in all conditions. This is because there is a smaller surface area for water to be lost from.	The student has described the results for temperature and stomatal density well, gaining 1 mark for each of these. While they did compare the data, they did not give the units, which meant they could not gain the mark for using data. The student has explained why the rate of transpiration is lower with fewer stomata, but they did not explain why the rate is lower on a hot day. They should have said that the stomata close to prevent excess water loss. *This answer is awarded 2 out of 3 marks.*

4 Now that you've gone through the commentary, try to write an improved answer to any part of question **3** where you did not score highly.

The following question has an example student response and commentary provided. Work through the question first, then compare your answer to the sample response and commentary. Are your answers different to the sample responses?

5 Fig. 5.1 shows part of a transverse section of a leaf.

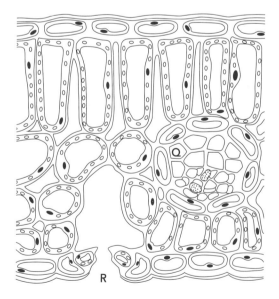

Fig. 5.1

a   Explain, in terms of water potential, how water moves from **Q** to **R**.   [4]

b   State and explain three ways in which the structure of xylem vessels
    is adapted to transport water.   [6]

[Total: 10]

Cambridge International AS & A Level Biology (9700) Paper 21, Q5, June 2009

Example student response	Commentary
5 a Water moves down a water potential gradient either by the apoplast pathway or symplast pathway. The water then evaporates and then moves out of the stomata.	The student has written a very good answer here, almost scoring full marks. They have correctly discussed movement according to water potential gradients and the two types of pathways. To gain the fourth mark they should have said water diffuses out of the stomata, instead of saying it moves out of the stomata. *This answer is awarded 3 out of 4 marks.*
b Thick cell wall to provide support. Lignin to waterproof and prevent water loss. There are perforated end walls to allow continuous flow of water.	The student has correctly stated and explained features. They lost 1 mark for incorrectly saying that there are perforated end walls. Xylem has no end walls; it is phloem that has perforated end walls. *This answer is awarded 5 out of 6 marks.*

6   Now that you've read the commentary, write a full mark scheme for question **5**.
    This will check that you've understood why each mark has (or has not)
    been allocated.

The following question has an example student response and commentary provided.
Work through the question first, then compare your answer to the sample response and
commentary. Are your answers different to the sample responses? Are there any areas
in which you feel you need to improve your understanding?

7   Fig. 7.1 is a diagram of a section through a mammalian heart.

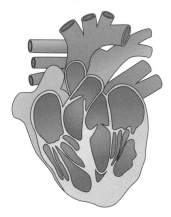

Fig. 7.1

a   Use a label line and the appropriate letter to label each of the following on Fig. 7.1:

W right atrium

X tricuspid valve

Y aorta   [3]

b   Starting from the left ventricle, describe the route taken by the blood as it travels to the lungs.   [3]

c   Describe and explain how the structure of the human gas exchange surface is adapted for maximum efficiency.   [4]

[Total: 10]

Cambridge International AS & A Level Biology (9700) Paper 23, Q4, November 2013

Example student response	Commentary
7 a	The student has correctly labelled the right atrium (**W**), tricuspid valve (**X**) and the aorta (**Y**). *This answer is awarded 3 out of 3 marks.*
b Blood flows out of the aorta to the rest of the body. The deoxygenated blood then re-enters the heart through the vena cava. The blood leaves the right ventricle and goes to the lungs. The oxygenated blood re-enters the heart into the left atrium.	The student has correctly gained marks for stating the blood leaves the aorta, goes to the body and re-enters through the vena cava. After this, the blood enters the right atrium, before entering the right ventricle, which the student missed out in their answer. The student correctly states that blood leaves the right ventricle to go towards the lungs, but they did not name the blood vessel (pulmonary vein) that this occurs through. They also did not state that blood enters the left atrium through the pulmonary artery. They should name the blood vessels through which blood enters and exits the heart. *This answer is awarded 2 out of 3 marks.*
c The lungs contain many alveoli which provide a large surface area for gas exchange.	The student correctly described and explained how the alveoli are adapted to increase gas exchange, but to answer the question fully the student should include more detail on the other structures of the lungs. For example, the student could have explained that the lungs have a large network of blood capillaries that maintain a diffusion gradient across the surface membrane of the alveoli. *This answer is awarded 2 out of 4 marks.*

Here is a similar question on the structure of the mammalian heart. Work through the question first, then compare your answer to the sample response and commentary. Are your answers different to the sample responses?

8   a   The thickness of the different chambers of the mammalian heart is due to the amount of cardiac muscle present. The atria have less cardiac muscle than the ventricles, and hence thinner walls.

In terms of their functions, explain why the atria have thinner walls than the ventricles.   [2]

   b   Name the dividing wall separating the right and left sides of the mammalian heart.   [1]

[Total: 3]

Cambridge International AS & A Level Biology (9700) Paper 22, Q6, November 2015

Example student response	Commentary
8 a The atria only have to pump the blood to the ventricles, which isn't very far. Therefore, they do not need a thick muscular layer.	The student has correctly explained why the atria have thinner walls, but they have not explained why the ventricles have thicker muscular walls. *This answer is awarded 1 out of 2 marks.*
b Purkyne fibres	The student is incorrect. The wall that separates the left and right sides is called the septum. The Purkyne fibres are located within the septum. *This answer is awarded 0 out of 1 mark.*

9   Now that you have read the student response and commentary, re-write your answer to any section in question **8** where you did not score highly. Use the commentary for guidance.

9 Gas exchange

It is important to revisit command words to gain practice answering questions across different topics and understand what level of depth is required in the answer. In this chapter, you will practise answering questions with the command words 'describe' and 'explain'. Use the knowledge and skills you have gained from working through Chapters 2 and 5 to support you. It is important that you understand what each command word is instructing you to do.

Describe	state the points of a topic or give characteristics and main features
Explain	set out purposes or reasons / make the relationships between things evident / provide why and/or how and support with relevant evidence

9.1 Gas exchange

1 What is the gas exchange surface in humans?

2 An individual alveolus is small, but there are on average 480 million alveoli in adult lungs. Explain the advantage of this. **[Total: 2]**

> **UNDERSTAND THESE TERMS**
> - gas exchange surface
> - alveolus
> - trachea
> - bronchus
> - bronchiole

9.2 Lungs

1 Label the thoracic cavity shown in Figure 9.1.

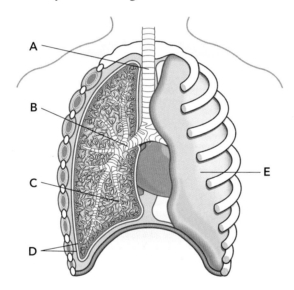

Figure 9.1: The thoracic cavity

2 Name the location where gas exchange occurs in humans. **[Total: 1]**

3 Name the airways that split from the bronchi. **[Total: 1]**

> **REFLECTION**
>
> The function of the gas exchange system and the circulatory system go hand in hand to enable oxygen to be delivered to respiring tissues and remove carbon dioxide. How many links can you make between the roles of the two systems? Try making a concept map to look at how these two systems work holistically.

9.3 Trachea, bronchi and bronchioles

1 Air passes through a series of tubes to reach the alveoli during ventilation. Name the three tubes and give the order that air would pass through them after entering through the nose or mouth.

2 How many bronchi do humans have?

3 Describe the role of cartilage in the trachea and bronchi. [Total: 2]

9.4 Warming and cleaning the air

1 The diameter of the bronchiole lumen can increase during exercise to increase the airflow to the alveoli. Give two adaptations why this is possible.

2 Describe how the air is warmed as it enters the body. [Total: 1]

3 Describe the role of the goblet and ciliated epithelial cells in cleaning the air. [Total: 4]

> **« RECALL AND CONNECT 2 «**
>
> Think back to Chapter 8 Transport in mammals: Describe how a red blood cell is adapted to maximise the transport of oxygen in the blood.

9.5 Alveoli

1 How is it possible for alveolar walls to stretch during inspiration and recoil during expiration?

2 State and explain three structural adaptations of the alveoli. [Total: 3]

SELF-ASSESSMENT CHECKLIST

Let's revisit the Knowledge focus and Exam skills focus for this chapter.

Decide how confident you are with each statement.

Now I can:	Show it	Needs more work	Almost there	Confident to move on
describe the structure of the human gas exchange system	Draw and label a diagram of the thoracic cavity.			
recognise the trachea, bronchi, bronchioles and alveoli in microscope slides, photomicrographs and electron micrographs and make plan diagrams of transverse sections of the walls of the trachea and bronchus	Search online for a micrograph of the human thoracic cavity. Use this image to draw a plan diagram of each of these stated structures and label them.			
describe and explain the distribution of tissues and cells within the gas exchange system and recognise them in microscope slides, photomicrographs and electron micrographs	Draw a plan diagram of the different tissues and cells in the gas exchange system.			
describe the functions in the gas exchange system of cartilage, smooth muscle, elastic fibres and squamous epithelium	Create a table to outline the structure and function of the cartilage, smooth muscle, elastic fibres and squamous epithelial cells.			
describe the functions of ciliated epithelial cells, goblet cells and mucous glands in maintaining the health of the gas exchange system	Write a paragraph to describe the function of each of these.			
describe gas exchange between air in the alveoli and blood in the capillaries	Create a flow diagram to describe the process of gas exchange.			

CONTINUED

Now I can:	Show it	Needs more work	Almost there	Confident to move on
understand the level of depth required in a 'describe' exam question compared with an 'explain' question	Write a 'describe' and an 'explain' question for this topic and suggest the number of marks they would be worth.			

10 Infectious disease

KNOWLEDGE FOCUS

In this chapter you will answer questions on:

- infectious disease
- antibiotics.

EXAM SKILLS FOCUS

In this chapter you will:

- check the quality of your answers, and look for gaps in knowledge.

In any topic, it is useful to review what you understand and check the quality of your answers. You can then determine what you need to do to improve. When answering 'describe' questions on the transmission of diseases you will need to include the main points or characteristics of how a disease is transmitted. Once you have answered the questions in this chapter, check your answers against the mark schemes. Then try again to get a perfect score.

10.1 Infectious disease

1   Copy and complete the table to show how these diseases are transmitted.

Disease	Mode of transmission
Cholera	
Malaria	

2   Describe how the transmission of malaria could be controlled.   **[Total: 3]**

3   Describe how tuberculosis (TB) is transmitted.   **[Total: 4]**

REFLECTION

How did you do on this four-mark question on how tuberculosis is transmitted? If you didn't gain full marks, review your answer and consider what was the reason you didn't achieve full marks. Was it the clarity in your answer, and you missed out key words? Was it that you couldn't remember the information? Or did you miss one of the marks? From this, set yourself a target to improve on the skill that was the reason for your lost mark(s).

≪ RECALL AND CONNECT 1 ≪

Think back to Chapter 1 Cell structure: Name two structures that are in a virus, but not in a bacterium.

10.2 Antibiotics

1   The effectiveness of antibiotics can be examined through inhibition zone plates. For example, in Figure 10.1, the bacterium *Escherichia coli* was grown with six antibiotic discs. Which antibiotic was the most effective at killing *Escherichia coli* and what is the evidence for this?

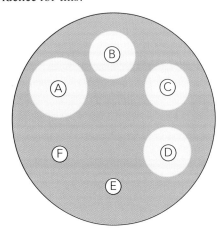

Figure 10.1: Inhibition zone plate with *Escherichia coli* grown with different antibiotic discs

2   Explain how the impact of antibiotic resistance can be reduced.   **[Total: 3]**

3   Describe how penicillin affects bacteria.   **[Total: 5]**

SELF-ASSESSMENT CHECKLIST

Let's revisit the Knowledge focus and Exam skills focus for this chapter.

Decide how confident you are with each statement.

Now I can:	Show it	Needs more work	Almost there	Confident to move on
explain that infectious diseases are caused by pathogens that are transmitted from person to person	Write a paragraph to explain how different pathogens discussed in this chapter are transmitted.			
give the names of the pathogens that cause cholera, malaria, tuberculosis (TB) and HIV/AIDS and explain how they are transmitted	Create flashcards with the name of the disease on one side and the pathogen that causes the disease on the other and test yourself.			
state that human pathogens can be viruses, bacteria and protoctists	For each of the named diseases, state which pathogen causes the disease.			
discuss the biological, social and economic factors that influence the effectiveness of control measures for cholera, malaria, TB and HIV	Create a table to outline the economic, social and biological effects of disease.			
outline the way in which the antibiotic penicillin acts on bacteria	Draw a bacterium and annotate your drawing with how penicillin can act on the bacterium.			
explain why antibiotics have no effect on viruses	Answer the question: 'Why can't antibiotics affect viruses?'			

CONTINUED

Now I can:	Show it	Needs more work	Almost there	Confident to move on
discuss the consequences of the resistance of pathogens to antibiotics	Write a paragraph to explain the consequences of antibiotic-resistant pathogens.			
outline the measures that can be taken to reduce the impact of antibiotic resistance	Create a list of ways in which antibiotic resistance could be reduced.			
check the quality of my answers, and look for gaps in knowledge	For any questions that you lose a mark on, analyse the reason. Was it knowledge, misreading the question or the clarity of your answer? Use this to set a target for how to improve.			

11 Immunity

You may think that short-answer and multiple choice questions can be answered in the same way. But you need to consider the differences between them. A multiple choice question has the correct answer given, but will contain a number of distractors – these are answers that may seem correct if you do not think about them properly.

Short-answer questions do not provide the correct answer but there is nothing to distract you away from the correct answer. So, multiple choice questions need to be answered using a different strategy.

If you can find the distractors first in a multiple choice question, working out the correct answer will be less difficult. There are some multiple choice questions in this chapter for you to practise – can you spot the distractors?

11.1 Defence against disease

1 What is meant by the term 'immune response'?

2 Give an example of an external defence and an internal
defence mechanism. **[Total: 2]**

≪ RECALL AND CONNECT 1 ≪

Think back to Chapter 3 Enzymes: How does a competitive inhibitor reduce
the rate of an enzyme-controlled reaction?

11.2 Cells of the immune system

1 Describe the process of phagocytosis. **[Total: 4]**

2 Explain why antibodies can bind to specific antigens on pathogens. **[Total: 3]**

3 Which events are part of the primary immune response?

I Memory cells divide into plasma cells.

II Plasma cells secrete antibodies.

III T-helper cells release cytokines.

A I and II   **B** II and III   **C** I and III   **D** I only   **[Total: 1]**

11.3 Active and passive immunity

1 When making monoclonal antibodies, plasma cells from the spleen of an animal
are fused with myeloma cells. What is the purpose of fusing plasma cells with
myeloma cells?

A To allow specific antibodies to be produced

B So the cells from the hybridoma can divide indefinitely

C To increase the rate of antibody production

D So the plasma cells are protected from changes caused by mutations

2 Define the term 'herd immunity'.

3 Describe the differences between active and passive immunity. **[Total: 5]**

4 What features of vaccination programs allow them to control diseases?

I They protect non-immunised members of a population from disease.

II They destroy the vector of diseases.

III They can prevent the spread of disease by creating ring immunity
in populations.

A I and II   **B** II and III   **C** I and III   **D** I only   **[Total: 1]**

UNDERSTAND THESE TERMS

- clonal selection
- clonal expansion
- plasma cell
- memory B cell
- primary immune response
- secondary immune response

REFLECTION

There were a few different question types in this chapter – did you recognise them all? Do you have different strategies in place for how to approach these different question types? How will you make sure you apply these strategies in the exam?

SELF-ASSESSMENT CHECKLIST

Let's revisit the Knowledge focus and Exam skills focus for this chapter.

Decide how confident you are with each statement.

Now I can:	Show it	Needs more work	Almost there	Confident to move on
describe the mode of action of macrophages and neutrophils	Create a flow diagram to show how both macrophages and neutrophils work.			
explain what is meant by the term 'antigen' and state the difference between self antigens and non-self antigens	Create a flashcard to define the term 'antigen' and create a comparison table for self and non-self antigens.			
describe what happens during a primary immune response and explain the role of memory cells in long-term immunity	Annotate a diagram outlining the B-lymphocyte and T-lymphocyte response to pathogens.			
explain how the molecular structure of antibodies is related to their functions	Draw and label an antibody, annotating how each feature relates to its function.			
outline the hybridoma method for the production of monoclonal antibodies and the principles of using monoclonal antibodies in the diagnosis and treatment of diseases	Create a flow diagram to show how hybridoma cells are made. List uses of monoclonal antibodies.			
describe the differences between the different types of immunity: active and passive and natural and artificial	Create a comparison table for active and passive immunity, and natural and artificial immunity.			

CONTINUED

Now I can:	Show it	Needs more work	Almost there	Confident to move on
explain that vaccines contain antigens that stimulate immune responses to provide long-term immunity and how vaccination programmes are used to control the spread of infectious diseases	Write a paragraph to explain how vaccines provide long-term immunity and protection for a population.			
consider the differences between short-answer and multiple choice questions	Go through a set of past papers and highlight the distractors in multiple choice questions.			

Exam practice 4

This section contains past paper questions from previous Cambridge exams, which draw together your knowledge on a range of topics that you have covered up to this point. These questions give you the opportunity to test your knowledge and understanding. Additional past paper practice questions can be found in the accompanying digital material.

The following question has an example student response and commentary provided. Work through the question first, then compare your answer to the sample response and commentary. Are your answers different to the sample responses?

1   Collagen is a major component of the cartilage found in some of the structures of the human gas exchange system. Cells that synthesise and secrete the components of cartilage are known as chondrocytes.

Fig. 1.1 is a transmission electron micrograph of a chondrocyte.

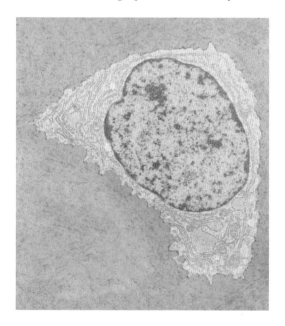

Fig. 1.1

a   With reference to Fig. 1.1, explain **two** features of the chondrocyte that show how the cell is adapted to its function.   [2]

b   i   Describe the distribution of cartilage in the human gas exchange system. [2]

    ii   Outline the function of cartilage in the human gas exchange system.   [2]

[Total: 6]

Cambridge International AS & A Level Biology (9700) Paper 22, Q4, June 2020

Example student response	Commentary
1 a It has lots of rough endoplasmic reticulum and mitochondria.	The student has correctly identified two features from the diagram, but the question asked them to explain two features. They should have explained that there is a lot of RER to synthesise collagen, which is a protein, and that there are lots of mitochondria to produce ATP for protein synthesis. *This answer is awarded 0 out of 2 marks.*
b i Cartilage is in the trachea and bronchi.	The student has correctly described which airway cartilage is located in. They could have also described that it occurs as C-shaped rings in the trachea. *This answer is awarded 2 out of 2 marks.*
ii It stops the airways from collapsing and closing when air pressure drops.	The student has given a correct answer, but an additional point is needed to gain both marks. They could have said that is provides support, or the C-shaped rings enable widening and flexibility during breathing and bending of the neck. *This answer is awarded 1 out of 2 marks.*

2 Now that you've gone through the commentary, try to write an improved answer to any part of question **1** where you did not score highly. This will help you check if you've understood why each mark has (or has not) been allocated.

Here is a similar question to question **1** that has an example student commentary and answer provided.

Work through the question first, then compare your answer to the sample response and commentary. Are your answers different to the sample responses? What information does this give you about your understanding of the topic?

3 Fig. 3.1 is a photomicrograph of epithelial cells in the bronchus.

    a i Write a letter **X** on Fig. 3.1 to show the lumen of the bronchus. [1]

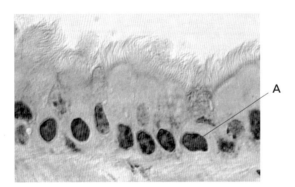

    Fig. 3.1

    ii Name the structure in Fig. 3.1 labelled **A**. [1]

    iii State **one** feature of the cells, visible in Fig. 3.1, which indicates that these are not epithelial cells from the alveolus. [1]

b Epithelial cells are replaced when they are damaged.

The cells shown in Fig. 3.1 are from a non-smoker.

Smoking causes damage to the epithelial cells of the lungs.

Describe the appearance of the lining of the bronchus
in a long-term smoker.   [4]

[Total: 7]

*Cambridge International AS & A Level Biology (9700) Paper 23, Q1a,bii,
June 2016*

Example student response	Commentary
3 a i	The student correctly labelled the diagram. *This answer is awarded 1 out of 1 mark.*
ii Vacuole	The student has incorrectly stated vacuole. *This answer is awarded 0 out of 1 mark.*
iii The cells are long and tall, rather than being thin and flat.	The student has correctly identified one feature. *This answer is awarded 1 out of 1 mark.*
b The bronchus lining would have fewer cilia and damaged cilia. There would also be a build-up of mucus because the cilia aren't there to sweep it out.	The student has correctly described two features. They needed to describe four features for the 4 marks. *This answer is awarded 2 out of 4 marks.*

4 Now attempt writing a full mark scheme for question **3 a iii** and part **b**, giving all
the possible correct answers.

The following question has an example student response and commentary provided. Work through the question first, then compare your answer to the sample response and commentary. Are your answers different to the sample responses? If they are, how are they different?

5   Cells of the immune system function to protect the body against infectious diseases.

   a   i   Name the type of cell that produces antibodies. [1]

      ii   The virus that causes the infectious disease influenza has two antigens, H and N. Antibodies are produced in response to an infection by this virus. The antibodies are specific for either antigen H or for antigen N.

         Describe how the structure of an antibody molecule allows it to be specific for one antigen, such as H or N. [3]

   b   Cholera is a disease caused by a bacterial pathogen.

      i   Name the pathogen that causes cholera. [1]

      ii   Describe how the pathogen that causes cholera is transmitted. [2]

   c   Viruses that infect bacteria are called bacteriophages. Some bacteriophages that infect the cholera pathogen cause lysis of the bacterium.

      i   Suggest what happens to the structure of a bacterial cell to cause lysis. [2]

      ii   Some scientists believe that bacteriophages could be used to treat people who are infected with cholera. Suggest the properties of the bacteriophages that would make this possible. [2]

      iii   Antibiotics can be used to treat people with cholera. State why antibiotics are not effective against measles. [1]

[Total: 12]

Cambridge International AS & A Level Biology (9700) Paper 21, Q3, November 2017

Example student response	Commentary
5 a i B cell	The student has not given a specific enough response here. *This answer is awarded 0 out of 1 mark.*
ii The variable region on an antigen is unique for each antibody. This unique shape is complementary in shape to only one antigen.	The student's first sentence is incorrect. The second sentence is correct but they could have also discussed what creates the unique complementary shape. *This answer is awarded 1 out of 3 marks.*
b i *Vibrio cholerae*	This answer is correct. *This answer is awarded 1 out of 1 mark.*
ii The pathogen will be in the faeces of someone who is infected with cholera. Someone becomes infected when they ingest the pathogen.	The student has the correct idea, but the answer is lacking detail and would not score any marks. The student would need to explain how water or food could be contaminated, and then state how an uninfected person becomes infected. *This answer is awarded 0 out of 2 marks.*

Example student response	Commentary
c i The cell wall of the bacteria would burst and break.	This answer is correct, but bacteria have a cell wall and a cell membrane, so the student should have also included that. *This answer is awarded 1 out of 2 marks.*
ii This would only be possible if the bacteriophage was specific to cholera bacteria and didn't infect humans.	The student has correctly identified one property, but they need to include a second property in order to score both marks. *This answer is awarded 1 out of 2 marks.*
iii Antibiotics are only effective against bacteria and cannot destroy viruses.	This is correct. *This answer is awarded 1 out of 1 mark.*

6 Now write an improved answer to the parts of question **5** where you lost marks.

The following question has an example student response and commentary provided. Work through the question first, then compare your answer to the sample response and commentary. Are your answers different to the sample responses?

7 Tuberculosis (TB) is an infectious disease caused by the bacterium *Mycobacterium tuberculosis*.

    a Describe how TB is transmitted. [2]

    b Streptomycin was the first antibiotic used to treat TB. Later, the antibiotic rifampicin was introduced as an alternative to streptomycin. Rifampicin acts by inhibiting the enzyme RNA polymerase. RNA polymerase is the enzyme used in transcription.

        i Explain what is meant by transcription. [2]

        ii *M. tuberculosis* and humans both use RNA polymerase for transcription. Suggest why rifampicin does not affect transcription in human cells. [1]

    c Other drugs such as isoniazid are also used in the treatment of TB. Some bacteria are now resistant to more than one of these drugs. These bacteria are known as multi-drug resistant (MDR) bacteria.

        Outline the steps that can be taken to reduce the impact of drug resistance in bacteria. [3]

    d Explain why antibiotics can be used to treat bacterial infections and not viral infections. [2]

[Total: 10]

Cambridge International AS & A Level Biology (9700) Paper 23, Q5a,c,d,e, June 2016

Example student response	Commentary
7 a An infected person coughs and transmits the bacteria this way.	The student would score 1 mark for this answer. To gain the second mark they could have stated it is a droplet infection and an uninfected person would inhale the droplets containing the bacteria. *This answer is awarded 1 out of 2 marks.*
b i Making mRNA from DNA	The student should specify that the mRNA is made from a DNA base sequence, which acts as a template. *This answer is awarded 1 out of 2 marks*
ii Because humans and bacteria have different physiologies	The student could have been more specific, stating that the RNA polymerase in the bacteria and humans must have a differently shaped active site. The student was too vague with this answer. *This answer is awarded 0 out of 1 mark.*
c To reduce the impact you could make sure patients complete the full course of antibiotics, stop the prophylactic use of antibiotics in agriculture and only have patients take antibiotics when it is absolutely necessary.	The student has given three valid reasons. *This answer is awarded 3 out of 3 marks.*
d Viruses are located inside of the host's cells so the antibiotic cannot reach them.	The student would score 1 mark for this, but they would need an additional reason. They could have also said that the antibiotics affect parts of the bacterial cell that are not present on a virus, such as the cell wall. *This answer is awarded 1 out of 2 marks.*

8   Now you have read the commentary, write an improved answer to the parts of question 7 where you lost marks. Use the commentary to guide you as you improve your answers.

The following question has an example student response and commentary provided. Work through the question first, then compare your answer to the sample response and commentary. Are your answers different to the sample responses?

9   T-helper lymphocytes and Leydig cells are two types of mammalian cells. The main role of T-helper lymphocytes and Leydig cells is to synthesise and secrete cell-signalling molecules.

- T-helper lymphocytes synthesise proteins known as cytokines.

- Leydig cells synthesise the steroid (lipid) hormone testosterone from cholesterol.

- Leydig cells also synthesise cholesterol.

a State **one** way in which cytokines are involved in an immune response. [1]

b Fig. 9.1 shows part of a mammalian cell.

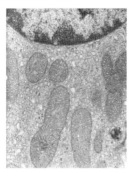

Fig. 9.1

i State, with reasons, whether Fig. 9.1 shows part of a Leydig cell or part of a T-helper lymphocyte. [2]

ii Underline the correct name for the type of image shown in Fig. 9.1 and explain your choice. [2]

- photomicrograph

- scanning electron micrograph

- transmission electron micrograph

c Testosterone molecules and cytokine molecules are transported in the circulatory system to reach their target cells. Testosterone molecules are able to enter their target cells and bind to receptors within the cytoplasm.

i Outline **one** way in which testosterone molecules could enter their target cells. [2]

ii Cytokine molecules are not able to enter their target cells. Suggest and explain why cytokine molecules are not able to cross the cell surface membrane to enter their target cells. [2]

[Total: 9]

Cambridge International AS & A Level Biology (9700) Paper 22, Q3, March 2021

Example student response	Commentary
9 a Cytokines stimulate the immune response.	The student has the correct idea, but must be more specific. They should have said that cytokines stimulate a response (either humoral or an example) with reference to B-lymphocytes. *This answer is awarded 0 out of 1 mark.*
b i It is a Leydig cell because it has lots of smooth endoplasmic reticulum.	The student correctly identified that it is a Leydig cell and that it has a lot of smooth endoplasmic reticulum. To gain the second mark, they needed to expand on their reason further and include the purpose of the smooth endoplasmic reticulum. *This answer is awarded 1 out of 2 marks.*

Example student response		Commentary
ii	Transmission electron micrograph; because there is a high resolution and you can see the ultrastructure.	The student has correctly identified the name for the image and given a full explanation for their choice. *This answer is awarded 2 out of 2 marks.*
c i	Testosterone could enter the cell by diffusion.	The student has given a correct method of how testosterone would enter, but they should have been more specific and included what it would diffuse through. *This answer is awarded 1 out of 2 marks.*
ii	Cytokine molecules must not be lipid soluble (hydrophilic) and so cannot diffuse across the membrane.	The student would score 1 mark for stating the cytokines are hydrophillic. They should have also suggested another reason that would prevent cytokine from passing through the membrane. *This answer is awarded 1 out of 2 marks.*

10 Now that you've gone through the commentary, have a go at writing a full mark scheme for question **9**. This will check that you've understood why each mark has (or has not) been allocated.

The following question has an example student response and commentary provided. Work through the question first, then compare your answer to the sample response and commentary. Are your answers different to the sample responses? Do you feel you need to improve your understanding of this topic?

11 Rheumatoid arthritis (RA) is a disease of the joints in the human body.

   a   RA is classed as an auto-immune disease where the immune system treats some self antigens as non-self.

   Explain what is meant by the term non-self antigens.   [3]

   b   The symptoms of RA include inflammation of the joints which causes pain and difficulty in movement of the joint. The inflammation is triggered by a chemical known as TNF-α, produced by macrophages.

   One approach to the treatment of RA is by the use of a monoclonal antibody against TNF-α.

   Fig. 11.1 is a diagram of an antibody molecule

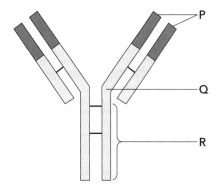

   Fig. 11.1

   i   Name the parts of the antibody molecule labelled **P**, **Q** and **R**.   [3]

   ii   Name the type of bonds that hold the polypeptide chains together in the antibody structure.   [1]

c i Outline how monoclonal antibody against TNF-α is produced. [3]

ii Suggest how monoclonal antibody against TNF-α can reduce the symptoms of RA. [2]

[Total: 12]

Cambridge International AS & A Level Biology (9700) Paper 23, Q4, June 2016

Example student response	Commentary
11 a A non-self antigen is foreign and not part of the person's body. It can therefore trigger an immune response.	The student has given a good answer. For the third mark, they should be more specific about what happens during the immune response. *This answer is awarded 2 out of 3 marks.*
b i P = variable region (the antigen-binding site) Q = hinge region R = constant region	The student has correctly identified the three labelled parts of the antibody. *This answer is awarded 3 out of 3 marks.*
ii Peptide bonds	The student incorrectly stated that peptide bonds hold the polypeptide chains together in antibodies. *This answer is awarded 0 out of 1 mark.*
c i The antigen would be added to a mouse, so that the mouse would make plasma cells for this antigen.	The student has correctly identified the first part of the process, but they needed to include the next part of the process to gain full marks. *This answer is awarded 2 out of 3 marks.*
ii The antibodies would bind and destroy the TNF-α.	The student needed to specify what exactly the antibodies would bind to. *This answer is awarded 1 out of 2 marks.*

12 Now write an improved answer to any part of question **11** where you did not score highly. You will need to carefully work back through each part of the question, ensuring that you include enough detail and clearly explain each point.

Practical skills for AS Level

Questions about practicals often require you to use and analyse data, and make calculations. It is important to show your workings in 'calculate' questions; as mentioned previously, you may be awarded marks for getting the method correct even if you arrive at the incorrect answer. Similarly, it is important to reference the data when, for example, giving conclusions or describing patterns.

P1.1 Practical skills

1 What is meant by a 'wet practical'?

2 In addition to wet practicals, give another example of a type of practical you may conduct.

≪ RECALL AND CONNECT 1 ≪

Why must large samples be taken in experiments?

P1.2 Experiments

1 Many wet practicals will involve investigating how one variable affects another variable.

State four variables that would affect the rate of an enzyme-controlled reaction. **[Total: 4]**

P1.3 Variables and making measurements

1 Explain why a control is used in experiments. **[Total: 2]**

P1.4 Recording quantitative results

1 A student was investigating the effect of pH on the enzyme amylase. Amylase, starch and iodine were mixed together in five different test tubes and five different pH buffers were added to each. They repeated each experiment three times. The time taken for the iodine to go from blue/black to orange was recorded.

Their results were:

pH 3 – 680 s, 700 s, 690 s

pH 5 – 430 s, 390 s, 400 s

pH 6 – 112 s, 120 s, 115 s

pH 7 – 100 s, 98 s, 97 s

pH 8 – 90 s, 70 s, 82 s

Design an appropriate table for these results.

UNDERSTAND THESE TERMS

- independent variable
- dependent variable
- standardised variables

UNDERSTAND THESE TERMS

- control
- accuracy
- precision
- replicates

« RECALL AND CONNECT 2 «

When plotting your data on a graph, which axes should the independent and dependent variables be plotted on?

P1.5 Displaying data

1   For each example of data, state the appropriate type of graph to use to display the data.

    a   Measuring the time taken for a reaction to occur at different temperatures.

    b   Recording the number of people who have the blood group A, B, AB or O.

    c   Recording how many petals different species of flowers have.

UNDERSTAND THESE TERMS

- discontinuous variable
- continuous variable

P1.6 Making conclusions

1   Give a conclusion for the data shown in the table.

Light intensity / lux	Average diameter of stomata / mm
10	0.01
20	0.09
30	0.15
40	0.83
50	1.02
60	1.09

[Total: 1]

P1.7 Describing data

1   With reference to the data shown in the table in question **1** in **P1.6**, describe the relationship between light intensity and the average diameter of the stomata.   [Total: 2]

P1.8 Making calculations from data

1   Calculate the mean time for each pH value in question **1** in **P1.4**.   [Total: 2]

Did you need to round your mean? To work out how many decimal points or significant figures you should round to in a table, look at how the rest of the data in the table is presented. You should be consistent and use the same format.

P1.9 Identifying sources of error and suggesting improvements

1   What is the difference between a systematic error and a random error?

P1.10 Drawings

1   What are the features of a scientific drawing?

2   How could the scientific drawing in Figure P1.1 be improved?

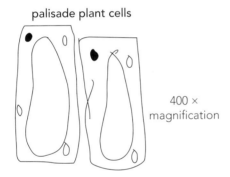

palisade plant cells

400 × magnification

Figure P1.1: A student's scientific drawing of two palisade cells

Let's revisit the Knowledge focus and Exam skills focus for this chapter.

Decide how confident you are with each statement.

Now I can:	Show it	Needs more work	Almost there	Confident to move on
collect data and observations	Record all qualitative and quantitative data in class practicals.			
make decisions about measurements and observations	Suggest which units would be most appropriate when measuring a mitochondrion under a microscope.			

CONTINUED

Now I can:	Show it	Needs more work	Almost there	Confident to move on
record data and observations appropriately	Design a table to collect the data for an experiment timing how long a reaction takes with six different concentrations of substrate.			
display calculations and reasoning clearly	Complete three calculations on experimental data, for example a statistic or mean, and show your workings.			
use tables and graphs to display data	Design a table to collect data for a class practical and once the data is collected, plot the data as a suitable graph.			
interpret data and observations	Complete three data analysis questions from a Practical paper 3.			
draw conclusions	Write a conclusion for all practical experiments you have conducted in class. Link to statistical data when they have been calculated.			
identify significant sources of error	Review the method of three practicals you have conducted in class and consider the limitations that might result in sources of error.			
suggest improvements to a procedure, or suggest how an investigation could be extended	Benedict's reagent can be used to test for reducing sugars and to estimate the concentration present. Suggest an improvement to this method to obtain more accurate results.			
understand the importance of showing my workings and use of data in questions about practicals	Look through some past-paper mark schemes; note the amount of 'method marks' given for calculate questions.			

12 Energy and respiration

Some exam questions will ask you to 'comment' on something. You need to give an informed opinion; in other words, an opinion based on your knowledge of the topic. Look to see how many marks the question is worth; this will give you an idea of how many points to make in your answer. Questions that require a 'comment' may also have a command word such as 'explain' or 'describe'.

12.1 The need for energy in living organisms

1   What are some main uses of energy in living organisms?

2   ATP molecules are made through phosphorylation.
    What are two ways in which phosphorylation can occur?

3   Explain why ATP is used as the universal energy currency.   **[Total: 3]**

≪ RECALL AND CONNECT 1 ≪

Think back to Chapter 6 Nucleic acids and protein synthesis: What are the three components of a DNA nucleotide? How is an RNA nucleotide different to a DNA nucleotide?

12.2 Aerobic respiration

1   How many carbon atoms are in each of the following molecules?

    a   Glucose

    b   Fructose phosphate

    c   Triose phosphate

    d   Pyruvate

    e   Acetyl group

    f   Citrate

    g   Oxaloacetate

2   Enzymes and coenzymes are essential for the reactions in aerobic respiration.

    a   Describe one difference between the roles of NAD and FAD to that
        of coenzyme A.   [1]

    b   NAD and FAD are involved in the Krebs cycle, which occurs in the matrix.
        ATP is produced in the matrix as well as the cristae.

        Explain how ATP is produced differently in the matrix compared with
        that at the cristae.   [2]

                                                                    [Total: 3]

≪ RECALL AND CONNECT 2 ≪

Think back to Chapter 3 Enzymes: What is an enzyme? How do enzymes work? Describe and explain how different factors affect the rate of enzyme activity. How are enzymes different from coenzymes structurally and functionally?

3   Oxidative phosphorylation takes place in the cristae of the mitochondria, as the final stage in aerobic respiration to produce ATP molecules, as shown in Figure 12.1.

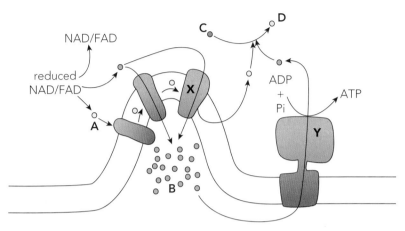

Figure 12.1

a   Identify the particles **A** and **B**.   [2]

b   Identify the processes **X** and **Y**.   [2]

c   State the role of chemical **C**. Suggest what would happen to the ATP synthase if chemical **C** were absent.   [4]

d   Some people are born with mitochondria that have extra proton channels in the cristae. Using this information, suggest why these people do not gain weight easily despite having a bigger appetite than others.   [4]

[Total: 12]

UNDERSTAND THESE TERMS
• chemiosmosis
• glycolysis
• decarboxylation
• dehydrogenation

REFLECTION

Were you able to recall the steps in aerobic respiration and to recall the various molecules involved in each reaction? It may be daunting to learn all the detailed steps in aerobic respiration, but can you think of a method to help you memorise them all? Remember that doing deliberate repeated practice of a well-planned diagram can help you form long-term memory of complicated steps and processes.

12.3 Mitochondrial structure and function

1   Which chemicals can diffuse through the outer membrane of mitochondria?

2   Why is it essential that mitochondria have their own DNA and ribosomes?

3   Aerobic respiration occurs in mitochondria, as shown in Figure 12.2.

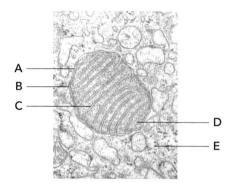

Figure 12.2

a   Using the letters **A–E** on Figure 12.2, identify the location(s) where each
    of the following reactions occurs.
    You may use each letter more than once.   [4]
    i   Link reaction
    ii   Glycolysis
    iii Electron transport chain
    iv   Krebs cycle

b   Explain the importance of **B** being folded.   [3]

c   A student says:
    'A cell can still produce ATP even if structure **A** of the mitochondria
    disappears.'
    Comment on whether or not the student is correct. Explain your reasons. [4]

[Total: 11]

12.4 Respiration without oxygen

1   Write **two** word equations to show how pyruvate is converted to ethanol
    in the two steps in ethanol fermentation.

2   Cells can respire anaerobically to keep generating ATP for survival.

    a   Compare the similarities and differences between the reactions
        of respiration in anaerobic conditions in mammals and yeast.   [4]

    b   Rice plants have adapted to survive in water, allowing them
        to outcompete weeds for resources for photosynthesis.
        Explain **two** adaptations of rice to allow it to grow well in water. [4]

[Total: 8]

> UNDERSTAND
> THESE TERMS
>
> • anaerobic
> • ethanol
>   fermentation
> • lactate
>   fermentation
> • aerenchyma

12.5 Respiratory substrates

1   Which component of a triglyceride allows it to release more energy than carbohydrates and proteins? Explain your answer.

2   The equation shows the breakdown of a substrate in aerobic respiration:

$$C_{55}H_{98}O_6 + 76.5\ O_2 \rightarrow 49\ H_2O + 55\ CO_2$$

Calculate the respiratory quotient (RQ) value of this substrate and identify the type of compound it is.

3   Student A set up an experiment to investigate the rate of respiration of germinating peas. As shown in Figure 12.3, they placed ten peas in each boiling tube and timed how long it took for the hydrogen carbonate indicator to change from pink to yellow.

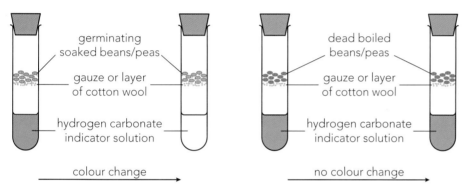

Figure 12.3

The hydrogen carbonate indicator solution is a pH indicator.
It is yellow when it is acidic and pink when it is alkaline.

a   Explain why the colour change of the indicator can be used to show respiration taking place.   [2]

b   Student A had another setup with boiled peas to act as a control setup. Student B said that this is not a reliable control. Comment on both students' decision.   [2]

c   Suggest one potential source of error in this experiment. Do not refer to human error in your answer.   [1]

d Student B did a similar experiment with a respirometer as shown in Figure 12.4. They repeated the experiment by placing four different peas into the respirometer to calculate their RQ values.

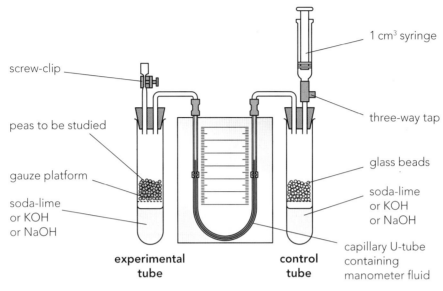

Figure 12.4

i Using Figure 12.4, explain one way this experiment is controlled. [2]

ii Suggest one other way the experiment can be improved for reliable results. [1]

iii By recording the liquid level in the capillary U-tube, student B could calculate the RQ values of four different pea species. The data are collated in the table.

Peas	RQ value
A	0.73
B	0.98
C	1.31
D	0.88

Using the data provided, comment on how each pea species is respiring. [4]

iv Student B says that these are estimated RQ values.

Suggest one reason why they are only estimated and not exact values. [1]

[Total: 13]

REFLECTION

How did you find the 'comment' questions in this chapter? Do you understand what you need to do? How will you remember how this differs from command words like 'discuss', 'explain', or 'suggest'?

UNDERSTAND THESE TERMS

- respiratory quotient (RQ)
- respirometer
- redox indicator

REFLECTION

There are many new key words and processes to learn in this chapter, so how have you helped yourself memorise all these details? What methods have you tried – what worked and what didn't? Consider what methods have helped you to memorise detailed processes from past chapters and see if you can use the same method to help you remember the processes in this chapter.

SELF-ASSESSMENT CHECKLIST

Let's revisit the Knowledge focus and Exam skills focus for this chapter.

Decide how confident you are with each statement.

Now I can:	Show it	Needs more work	Almost there	Confident to move on
outline the need for energy in living organisms	List the uses of energy in living organisms.			
explain how ATP is suited for the role as the universal energy currency	Draw an annotated diagram of an ATP molecule and list its properties.			
describe how ATP is synthesised	State the way in which ADP can be phosphorylated to make ATP.			
describe the stages in aerobic respiration – glycolysis, the link reaction, the Krebs cycle and oxidative phosphorylation – including the roles of NAD, FAD and coenzyme A	Draw a detailed diagram or flowchart to show the whole process of respiration, including the names of all substrates and additional molecules.			
describe the relationship between structure and function of mitochondria	Draw a labelled diagram of a mitochondrion, including the names, functions and adaptations of each of its structures.			
outline lactate fermentation and ethanol formation to provide a small quantity of ATP in anaerobic conditions	Find how many ATP, reduced NAD and FAD molecules are made under anaerobic conditions and compare this to that of aerobic respiration.			

CONTINUED

Now I can:	Show it	Needs more work	Almost there	Confident to move on
explain how rice is adapted to grow with its roots submerged in water	List the adaptations of rice and explain each.			
compare the energy values of different respiratory substrates	State which respiratory substrate gives the highest energy, and which gives the lowest energy. Explain.			
calculate respiratory quotients	Write down the equation for calculating RQ.			
describe how to carry out investigations using respirometers	Describe how oxygen uptake is measured using a respirometer and explain how external conditions can be controlled. State the chemical that is used to absorb carbon dioxide in the respirometer.			
describe how to carry out investigations using redox indicators	Explain how redox indicators (for example DCPIP) can change colour and how this can be used to measure the rate of respiration.			
show that I understand how to answer questions that ask me to 'comment' on something	Explain to someone what 'comment' means and write an example 'comment' question and answer.			

13 Photosynthesis

Biology is holistic and, although you are taught the theory in separate lessons, all the topics and concepts connect. Synoptic questions require you to demonstrate knowledge of different topics, and the connections between them. Before you start answering synoptic questions, list the relevant, overlapping topics. For example, there are strong links between the concepts in this chapter, and those covered as part of Chapter 1: Cell structure and Chapter 12: Energy and respiration. As you work through the questions in this chapter, see if you can spot the synoptic questions and think carefully about how best to answer them.

The Exam skills chapter at the beginning of this book has more support and suggestions for how to learn to recognise and use synoptic links between topics.

13.1 An energy transfer process

1 Which term is being described in each of the following descriptions?

   a   The first stage of photosynthesis that requires light

   b   The second and final stage of photosynthesis that does not require light

   c   Using light to split water

   d   Using light to produce ATP

   e   The proton carrier involved in photosynthesis

2 Copy and complete the paragraph that summarises the process of photosynthesis using appropriate terms.

   Photosynthesis is a reaction that takes place in organisms that have the organelles
   .... This organelle contains a green pigment called .... that
   absorbs light energy for the reaction to occur. Part of this light energy is used
   in a reaction called .... , which splits water molecules into hydrogen and
   oxygen. The hydrogen then contributes to ATP production through ....
   and reduces a coenzyme called .... , which is then used to produce
   carbohydrates as the final product.

   [Total: 5]

UNDERSTAND THESE TERMS
• chlorophyll
• photolysis
• photophosphorylation
• NADP

13.2 Structure and function of chloroplasts

1 What are the four examples of photosynthetic pigments?

2 How are photosynthetic pigments arranged in the thylakoid membrane?

3 What is the difference between an absorption spectrum and an action spectrum?

4 How might an absorption spectrum and an action spectrum be related?

5   Figure 13.1 shows a micrograph of a chloroplast.

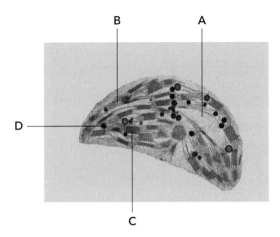

Figure 13.1

a   State the type of microscope that was used to view this chloroplast.
    Explain your choice.   [2]
b   State the names of structures **A–D**.   [4]
c   Using Figure 13.1 describe one similarity and one difference between
    the structures of chloroplasts and mitochondria.   [2]

[Total: 8]

> **UNDERSTAND THESE TERMS**
> - absorption spectrum
> - photosystem
> - chromatography
> - R_f value
> - action spectrum

≪ RECALL AND CONNECT 1 ≪

Think back to Chapter 12 Energy and respiration: What are the structural features of a mitochondrion? What does each part do?

13.3 The light-dependent stage of photosynthesis

1   What are the differences between cyclic and non-cyclic photophosphorylation?

2   What are the end products of the light-dependent stage of photosynthesis?

3   During the light-dependent stage of photosynthesis, the two photosystems
    absorb light to excite the electrons to go through the electron transport chain.
    Due to the fluctuations of the energy levels in electrons, this stage is also
    known as the Z-scheme.

a   State the exact location where the light-dependent stage occurs. [1]
b   Explain how photosystem II is adapted to excite electrons.   [4]
c   ATP is produced during this stage by photophosphorylation.
    Describe the similarities and differences between photophosphorylation
    and oxidative phosphorylation in aerobic respiration.   [4]

[Total: 9]

> **UNDERSTAND THESE TERMS**
> - cyclic photo-phosphorylation
> - photoactivation
> - non-cyclic photo-phosphorylation
> - oxygen-evolving complex

13.4 The light-independent stage of photosynthesis

1   What is the enzyme that fixes carbon dioxide into the substrates?

2   The Calvin cycle uses the products from the light-dependent stage to make carbohydrates.

   a   Describe and explain how the Calvin cycle produces carbohydrates.   [6]

   b   Although the Calvin cycle does not require light to occur, the rate of its reactions may decrease at night. Suggest why.   [4]

   c   The Calvin cycle can also produce proteins using its substrates and mineral ions from the soil. Suggest one mineral ion that is needed to produce proteins from the Calvin cycle and explain your choice.   [3]

   [Total: 13]

REFLECTION

How did you find question **2a** in this section? Did you make a note of the marks available to ensure you made enough points? How confident are you that you understand what these command words mean?

---

3   Photorespiration is a process where RuBP is converted into 2-phosphoglycolate. It is more likely to occur when there is a high level of oxygen and where the conditions are hot and dry.

   Using Figure 13.2, suggest how high concentrations of oxygen can cause photorespiration to occur and why this is undesirable for farmers.   **[Total: 4]**

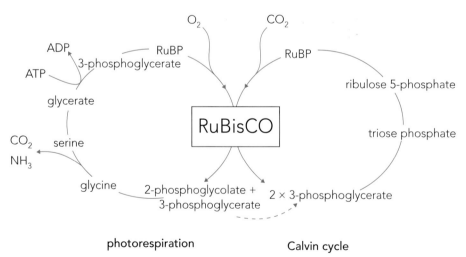

Figure 13.2

UNDERSTAND THESE TERMS

- ribulose bisphosphate (RuBP)
- RuBisCO
- glycerate-3-phosphate (GP)
- triose phosphate (TP)

13.5 Limiting factors in photosynthesis

1 List four environmental factors that affect photosynthesis.

2 A student investigated how light intensity affects the rate of carbon dioxide uptake between a plant and its environment, as shown in Figure 13.3.

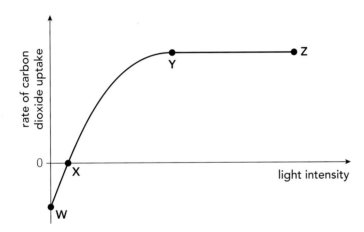

Figure 13.3

a Describe and explain how the rate of carbon dioxide uptake changes between points **X**, **Y** and **Z**. [5]

b Suggest what is happening between points **W** and **X**. Explain your answer. [2]

c The student did the experiment at 15 °C. Draw a line on a copy of Figure 13.3 to show what the graph may look like if the experiment was conducted at 25 °C. [1]

d Apart from temperature, State a limiting factor between points:

i **X** and **Y**

ii **Y** and **Z** [2]

[**Total: 10**]

3   A student investigated how the wavelength of light (colour) affects photosynthesis. They prepared four tubes of chloroplast suspension from the same plant and added a redox indicator called DCPIP into each tube. Three tubes were then placed under red, green and blue light, respectively. One tube was placed in the dark. The student then recorded any colour change seen after 5 minutes.

DCPIP is blue when oxidised and colourless when reduced.

The results are summarised in the table.

Colour of the light	Initial colour of mixture	Final colour of mixture
No light	Blue-green	Blue-green
Red	Blue-green	Green with a little blue
Green	Blue-green	Blue-green
Blue	Blue-green	Green

a   Suggest two factors that should be controlled in this experiment.   [2]

b   Suggest why one chloroplast–DCPIP mixture was placed in the dark.   [1]

c   The student then interpreted the results to determine the effects of light colour on photosynthesis.

   i   Using the table, identify and explain which colour of light has the greatest effect on the rate of photosynthesis.   [3]

   ii   Explain why the chloroplasts in the suspension appear green before adding DCPIP.   [1]

d   Another student replicated this experiment but used a homogenised solution of plant cells instead. The solution contained all the organelles in the plant cells released from the cytoplasm without being destroyed.

   After 5 minutes, the student saw that all four tubes had turned green.

   Suggest why.   [2]

[Total: 9]

UNDERSTAND
THIS TERM

- limiting factor

REFLECTION

Sometimes you get synoptic exam questions. These are questions that test you on knowledge from different topics and to see if you can form links in between to give a good answer. Could you spot some examples of such questions in this chapter? What can you do in your own revision to help you prepare for synoptic questions?

SELF-ASSESSMENT CHECKLIST

Let's revisit the Knowledge focus and Exam skills focus for this chapter.

Decide how confident you are with each statement.

Now I can:	Show it	Needs more work	Almost there	Confident to move on
explain how photosynthesis transfers energy from light to carbohydrate molecules	Describe what plants have that allow them to absorb light for photosynthesis.			
explain how the structure of a chloroplast is related to its functions	Draw a diagram of a chloroplast and annotate it with its structures and functions of each part.			
describe the roles of chloroplast pigments, and interpret absorption spectra and action spectra	State four examples of photosynthetic pigments and describe what absorption spectra and action spectra are.			
describe how to use chromatography to separate chloroplast pigments and calculate R_f values	Draw an annotated diagram of a setup of chromatography and write down the equation to calculate R_f values.			
describe the reactions of the light-dependent stage of photosynthesis, including cyclic photophosphorylation and non-cyclic photophosphorylation	Draw a detailed diagram showing how the light-dependent stage occurs, including all the substrates and molecules involved.			
describe the light-independent stage of photosynthesis	Draw a detailed diagram showing how the light-independent stage occurs, including all the substrates and molecules involved.			
explain the main limiting factors for photosynthesis, and interpret graphs showing the effects of these on the rate of photosynthesis	Sketch a graph for each limiting factor, showing how they affect the rate of photosynthesis.			

CONTINUED

Now I can:	Show it	Needs more work	Almost there	Confident to move on
describe how to investigate the effects of limiting factors on the rate of photosynthesis using aquatic plants	Write a step-by-step method to illustrate how to investigate the effect of one limiting factor on the rate of photosynthesis, including all variables and a description of how you would measure the results.			
describe how to investigate the effect of light intensity and light wavelengths on a chloroplast suspension, using a redox indicator	Write a step-by-step method to illustrate how to investigate the effect of light intensity and wavelength on photosynthesis, including the name of the redox indicator you would use and how to vary light intensity and wavelength.			
answer synoptic questions	Draw a mind map to illustrate as many links as you can find between photosynthesis and other topics.			

Exam practice 5

This section contains past paper questions from previous Cambridge exams, which draw together your knowledge on a range of topics that you have covered up to this point. These questions give you the opportunity to test your knowledge and understanding. Additional past paper practice questions can be found in the accompanying digital material.

The following question has an example student response and commentary provided. Work through the question first, then compare your answer to the sample response and commentary. Are your answers different to the sample responses?

1 Structures and compounds involved in respiration in anaerobic conditions include:

A pyruvate	**F** NAD
B reduced NAD	**G** ethanal
C ethanol	**H** lactate
D carbon dioxide	**I** oxygen
E cytoplasm	**J** mitochondrion

Complete Table 1.1 by matching each description with **one** letter chosen from **A** to **J** to show the correct structure or compound.

You may use each letter once, more than once or not at all. **[Total: 6]**

Description	Letter
end product of glycolysis	
cellular location of respiration in anaerobic conditions	
end product of respiration in anaerobic conditions in yeast cells	
compound used to reduce pyruvate	
end product of respiration in anaerobic conditions in muscle cells	
gas released during alcoholic fermentation	

Table 1.1

Cambridge International AS & A Level Biology (9700) Paper 41, Q7a, November 2020

Example student response		Commentary
1		The answer for 'compound used to reduce pyruvate' should be B – reduced NAD.

description	letter
end product of glycolysis	A
cellular location of respiration in anaerobic conditions	E
end product of respiration in anaerobic conditions in yeast cells	C
compound used to reduce pyruvate	F
end product of respiration in anaerobic conditions in muscle cells	H, D
gas released during alcoholic fermentation	D

Pyruvate is reduced by gaining hydrogen from a reduced NAD.

Remember that only the first answer is accepted in each box unless otherwise specified. If the correct answer is given but is followed with an incorrect answer, it will also negate the mark – so an answer of 'H, D' will be awarded no marks.

This answer is awarded 4 out of 6 marks.

Now attempt an additional question. Use the previous commentary to guide you as you answer this question.

2 a The link reaction and Krebs cycle take place in the mitochondrion.

The main stages of the link reaction and Krebs cycle are listed in Table 2.1.

They are **not** listed in the correct order.

stage	description of stage
A	acetyl group combines with coenzyme A to form acetyl CoA
B	citrate is formed
C	hydrogen atoms are accepted by NAD and FAD
D	oxaloacetate is regenerated
E	pyruvate enters the mitochondrial matrix
F	acetyl group is formed
G	acetyl CoA enters Krebs cycle
H	ATP is made by substrate-linked phosphorylation
I	pyruvate is decarboxylated and dehydrogenated
J	acetyl CoA combines with oxaloacetate
K	citrate is decarboxylated and dehydrogenated

Table 2.1

Complete Table 2.2 to show the correct order of the stages.

Three of the stages have been done for you.

correct order	letter of stage
1	E
2	
3	
4	
5	
6	J
7	
8	
9	
10	
11	D

[4]

Table 2.2

b   Outline the role of NAD in respiration in aerobic conditions.   [4]

c   Carbon dioxide is removed from compounds in the link reaction
and Krebs cycle by decarboxylation.

    i   State the total number of molecules of carbon dioxide removed
in the link reaction and Krebs cycle for each molecule of glucose
respired.   [1]

    ii   In a mammal, carbon dioxide diffuses from cells into the blood
to be transported to the lungs. Suggest why carbon dioxide is
transported in the blood mainly as hydrogen carbonate ions
and not as carbonic acid.   [1]

[Total: 10]

Cambridge International AS & A Level Biology (9700) Paper 41, Q4, June 2019

The following question has an example student response and commentary provided. Work through the question first, then compare your answer to the sample response and commentary. Are your answers different to the sample responses? What information does this give you about your understanding of this topic?

CAMBRIDGE INTERNATIONAL AS & A LEVEL BIOLOGY: EXAM PREPARATION AND PRACTICE

3 **a** Fig. 3.1 is a transmission electron micrograph of a chloroplast.

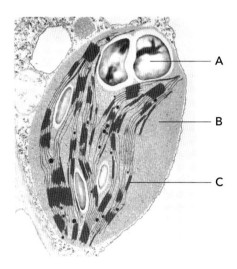

Fig. 3.1

Many compounds and structures involved in photosynthesis are located in a chloroplast.

Using the labels **A**, **B** or **C**, complete Table 3.1 to show the location of four of these compounds or structures.

You may use each of the letters **A**, **B** and **C** once, more than once or not at all.

compound or structure	location
ATP synthase	
RuBisCO	
starch grain	
phospholipid bilayer	

[3]

Table 3.1

b *Elodea canadensis* is an aquatic plant that lives submerged in freshwater.

Equal-sized plants of *E. canadensis* were exposed to different wavelengths of light for the same period of time. As each plant photosynthesised, the number of bubbles of oxygen leaving the plant was counted.

For each wavelength, the rate of oxygen production was calculated.

The results are shown in Fig. 3.2.

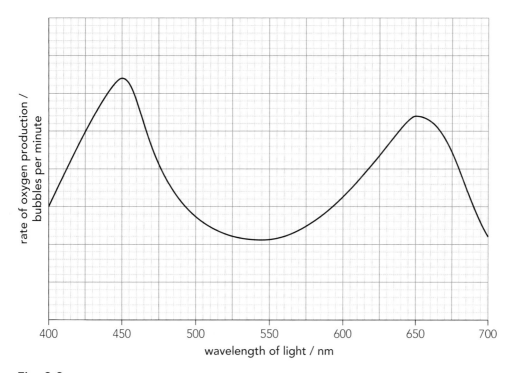

Fig. 3.2

Describe **and** explain the results shown in Fig. 3.2.   [3]

c Chlorophyll *b*, carotene and xanthophyll are known as accessory pigments. Describe the role of the accessory pigments in photosynthesis.   [2]

[Total: 8]

Cambridge International AS & A Level Biology (9700) Paper 41, Q7, November 2018

Example student response	Commentary
3 a 	compound or structure	location	 	ATP synthase	C	 	RuBisCO	B	 	starch grain	A	 	phospholipid bilayer	C		The student has correctly identified the structures in the chloroplast and has a clear understanding of the processes in each location within the chloroplast. *This answer is awarded 3 out of 3 marks.*
b The rate of oxygen production peaks at wavelengths of 450 nm and 650 nm. This means the rate of photosynthesis is the highest at those two wavelengths. This is due to the photosynthetic pigments being able to absorb those wavelengths better than other wavelengths.	The student correctly describes the trend shown in the graph, identifying the wavelengths of light that increase the rate of oxygen production. They also correlated this to the rate of photosynthesis, interpreting what the graph shows. There is also an attempt to give an explanation to the description, which is what the question asked for. However, the student has not explained how the light is used to produce oxygen in the plant, which is what the question was looking for. *This answer is awarded 2 out of 3 marks.*
c They absorb other wavelengths of light, different from chlorophyll *a*.	The student recognises that accessory pigments absorb different wavelengths of light compared with the primary pigment but has not included sufficient detail for 2 marks. The answer should also refer to how the accessory pigments interact with the primary pigment and their involvement in photosynthesis, for example channelling energy harvested from light to the chlorophyll *a* molecules, which increases the energy in the chlorophyll *a* molecules. *This answer is awarded 1 out of 2 marks.*

Now attempt the following additional question. Use the previous sample answers and commentaries to guide you as you answer.

4 a Describe the process of **cyclic** photophosphorylation **and** the structure of the photosystem involved. [9]

b Explain how **non-cyclic** photophosphorylation produces reduced NADP **and** how reduced NADP is used in the light independent stage. [6]

[Total: 15]

Cambridge International AS & A Level Biology (9700) Paper 42, Q9, March 2018

14 Homeostasis

In this chapter, you will practise how to form long-response answers. These questions usually require detailed knowledge of the content. You need to be able to show your understanding in a logical and organised way to answer long-response questions. This requires planning. Annotating exam questions and making lists of key words and phrases will help to ensure you can give a concise, organised answer with the necessary details, without wasting time by including unnecessary details or introductions.

14.1 Homeostasis

1 What is the difference between the three nitrogenous wastes: urea, creatinine and uric acid?

2 The internal conditions in mammals fluctuate throughout a day, which can be caused by metabolic reactions and external stimuli. It is essential that such conditions are regulated carefully through negative feedback.

    a Explain why each condition must be controlled at a set point.

        i Water potential in blood [2]

        ii Blood glucose concentration [2]

    b Digestion is an example of metabolic reactions. Various food molecules are broken down and absorbed in digestion, such as proteins.

        i State the name of the enzyme that digests proteins. [1]

        ii Excess amino acids are produced from the breakdown of proteins. Name the substance that is produced from excess amino acids and state the location where the production takes place. [2]

[Total: 7]

> **UNDERSTAND THESE TERMS**
> - homeostasis
> - negative feedback
> - urea
> - excretion
> - deamination

14.2 The structure of the kidney

1 What structures in the nephron act as filters in the process of ultrafiltration? What substances do they filter?

2 How is the nephron structured to generate a filtration pressure difference in the glomerulus?

3 The kidney is made up of nephrons.

    a Figure 14.1 shows the structure of a mammalian nephron.

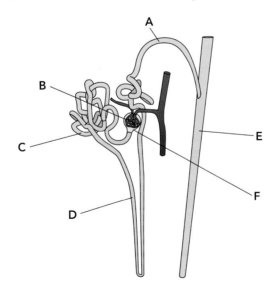

Figure 14.1

Using the letters **A–F** in Figure 14.1, determine which structure(s) carries out the following processes.

You may use each letter once, more than once or not at all.

There may be more than one answer for each process.   [3]

Process	Structure
Ultrafiltration	
Reabsorption of glucose	
Osmoregulation	

b   Identify structure **B** and explain how it is adapted for its function.   [3]

[Total: 6]

4   Different solutes are selectively reabsorbed back into the bloodstream in the kidneys. Most of this process occurs in the proximal convoluted tubule.

Explain three adaptations of the proximal convoluted tubule that allow it to reabsorb various solutes into the body.   **[Total: 7]**

≪ RECALL AND CONNECT 1 ≪

Think back to Chapter 4 Cell membranes and transport: What are the different mechanisms of transport in and out of cells? Give the definition of each mechanism.

UNDERSTAND THESE TERMS

- nephron
- glomerulus
- afferent arteriole
- efferent arteriole
- podocyte

14.3 Control of water content

UNDERSTAND THESE TERMS

- osmoregulation
- osmoreceptor

1   State the receptor, coordinator and effector in the control of blood water level.

2   Describe and explain how an increase in anti-diuretic hormone (ADH) causes a change in urine production in the nephron.   **[Total: 6]**

14.4 The control of blood glucose

1 Copy and complete the table to summarise how the body regulates blood glucose concentration (BGC).

	To increase BGC	To decrease BGC
Hormone		
Chemical reactions in the target cell		

2 What is the end result of the action of the enzyme, protein kinase A? Does it increase or decrease BGC?

3 Blood glucose level is regulated by the pancreas.

a In order to decrease blood glucose level, muscle cells would absorb glucose at a faster rate and convert it into glycogen.

    i Describe the structure of glycogen. [3]

    ii Explain the importance of the conversion of glucose to glycogen. [2]

    iii In contrast with insulin, glucagon binds to the receptors of liver cells to cause an enzyme cascade that ultimately decreases the blood glucose level.

        Outline how glucagon triggers the enzyme cascade and explain its significance. [6]

b People with diabetes cannot regulate their blood glucose level easily and may excrete excess glucose in their urine. As a result, detecting glucose levels in urine became a method for diagnosing diabetes. This can be done by using glucose test strips or a biosensor.

    For both methods, enzymes are used in detecting the presence of glucose.

    i State the names of the two enzymes that are used in test strips. Describe the reactions they catalyse for detecting glucose. [4]

    ii A student claims:

        'Biosensors are more accurate in diagnosing diabetes than test strips.'

        Using your understanding of how biosensors work, give a reason for the student's claim. [4]

[Total: 19]

UNDERSTAND THESE TERMS

- glycogenesis
- glycogenolysis
- gluconeogenesis
- adenylyl cyclase
- protein kinase A

≪ RECALL AND CONNECT 2 ≪

Think back to Chapter 2 Biological molecules: Apart from glycogen, what other polysaccharides are there? Describe their structures and functions.

14.5 Homeostasis in plants

1 Under what conditions would stomata close?

2 List the ions that are involved in regulating stomatal opening and closure.

3 Guard cells are specialised plant cells that regulate the opening and closing of stomata.

    a Explain how guard cells are adapted for this function. [4]

    b Copy and complete the flowchart in Figure 14.2 to illustrate the process of stomatal opening. [4]

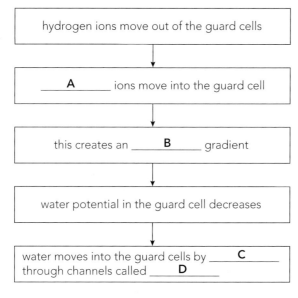

Figure 14.2

    c The plant may experience water stress after the stomata have been open for long periods of time. A plant hormone is released in response to this.

      i Name the plant hormone that is released in response to water stress. [1]

      ii This hormone causes a series of actions in the guard cells to close the stomata. Several ions are involved in this.

        Describe how these ions causes stomatal closure. [6]

[Total: 15]

4   Plants regulate their stomatal opening and closing at a daily rhythm. A student measured the stomatal aperture over time with light and darkness. The results are plotted in a graph as shown in Figure 14.3. Black bands indicate moments when the plant was in total darkness. The moments with no bands indicate when the plant was in light.

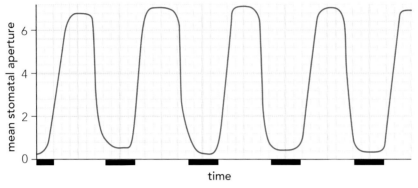

Figure 14.3

a   Explain how this graph illustrates the importance of a plant's ability to regulate its stomatal opening.   [5]

b   The student repeated the experiment with the same plant, but they kept it in the light throughout this time. The results are shown in Figure 14.4.

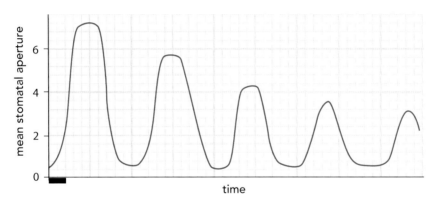

Figure 14.4

i   Describe the pattern of stomatal aperture shown in Figure 14.4.   [2]

ii   Suggest reasons for the pattern shown.   [3]

[Total: 10]

UNDERSTAND THESE TERMS

- guard cell
- electrochemical gradient
- abscisic acid (ABA)

REFLECTION

Some exam questions require a longer response than others and often are worth more marks. They test your subject understanding, application of knowledge and your ability to write an organised answer. How can you approach such questions without spending too much time on them in proportion to the rest of the exam paper? What should you look out for when reading and interpreting these questions, and how can you organise your answers?

SELF-ASSESSMENT CHECKLIST

Let's revisit the Knowledge focus and Exam skills focus for this chapter.

Decide how confident you are with each statement.

Now I can:	Show it	Needs more work	Almost there	Confident to move on
explain the meaning of the term 'homeostasis' and explain why homeostasis is important for mammals	Define the word 'homeostasis' and give examples of internal conditions that need such control and regulation.			
explain the principles of homeostasis in terms of: stimuli, receptors, effectors and the way in which responses are coordinated by the nervous and endocrine systems	Draw a flowchart to show how the different components in the pathway join up to coordinate responses. Give examples of receptors, coordinators and effectors in the nervous and endocrine systems.			
explain how negative feedback is involved in homeostatic mechanisms	Define the term 'negative feedback' and give examples.			
state that urea is produced by deamination of excess amino acids in the liver	Draw the structure of an amino acid and annotate it to show which part is removed by deamination to produce urea and other products.			
describe the structure of the human kidney and identify in diagrams the parts of a nephron and its associated blood vessels	Draw or print a large diagram of a nephron and label the structures.			
describe and explain how urine is formed in nephrons	On the same nephron diagram, add arrows and annotations to each part of the nephron to show what substances are reabsorbed into the bloodstream, including the mechanisms of transport.			

CONTINUED

Now I can:	Show it	Needs more work	Almost there	Confident to move on
describe the detailed structure of the Bowman's capsule and proximal convoluted tubule and explain how they are adapted for ultrafiltration and selective reabsorption	Draw a table and in one of the columns, list the structures and adaptations found in the Bowman's capsule and the proximal convoluted tubule. In the next column, give a reason why that adaptation supports its function.			
describe how the kidneys control the water potential of the blood and explain how osmoregulation is coordinated	Draw a flowchart with a 'normal water potential' in the middle line (as the set point), and an arrow going above and another going below the line. Add descriptions following the arrows to show the steps in osmoregulation to bring the water potential back to the set point (middle line).			
describe the principles of cell signalling as applied to the control of blood glucose concentration by glucagon	Draw a diagram to show how glucagon binding to cell surface receptors would bring about the enzyme cascade to increase blood glucose level.			
explain how blood glucose concentration is controlled	Draw a flowchart with a 'normal blood glucose level' in the middle line (as the set point), and an arrow going above and another going below the line. Add descriptions following the arrows to show the actions of insulin and glucagon on how they bring the blood glucose level back to the set point (middle line).			
explain how test strips and biosensors are used for measuring the concentration of glucose in blood and urine and explain the roles of glucose oxidase and peroxidase enzymes	Draw a table to compare test strips and biosensors, including how they work, their advantages and potential disadvantages.			

CONTINUED

Now I can:	Show it	Needs more work	Almost there	Confident to move on
describe the structure and function of guard cells and explain how they regulate the width of the stomatal aperture	Draw two diagrams – one of an open stoma and another of a closed one, with the guard cells around them. Annotate the diagrams to describe the state of the guard cells and the environmental conditions they would be in.			
explain that stomata control the entry of carbon dioxide by diffusion and regulate water loss by transpiration, thus balancing the needs for photosynthesis and conservation of water	Draw a diagram of an open stoma and add arrows to show what substances can enter and leave the stoma. Add further arrows or label lines to indicate the use of each substance.			
explain that stomata have daily rhythms of opening and closing and respond to changes in environmental conditions	Sketch a graph to show stomatal aperture over 48 hours. Add descriptions to each part of the graph to explain what is happening to the plant in response to stomatal opening/closing.			
describe how abscisic acid is involved in the closure of stomata during times of water shortage	Draw a diagram of an open stoma with an ABA molecule bound to a receptor. Add arrows and labels to the diagram to show the subsequent events after binding.			
structure long-form responses and plan my response before writing	Read and annotate a six-mark question to see what it is asking of you. Highlight any key information provided in the question, then list the key words or concepts that you should include in your final answer.			

15 Control and coordination

Remember that 'identify' is often used with questions that have diagrams, figures or graphs and is instructing you to look at these to help you as you answer. If you are asked to 'identify' a certain number of choices, you should be careful not to provide more responses than requested.

Identify	name/select/recognise

15.1 Hormonal communication

1 Copy and complete the table to name some endocrine glands and the hormones they release.

Endocrine gland	Hormone(s)	Peptide hormone or steroid hormone?
	ADH	
	Insulin and glucagon	

2 Describe how the endocrine system affects the functions of organs. Include the hormones insulin, glucagon and ADH as examples in your answer. **[Total: 8]**

≪ RECALL AND CONNECT 1 ≪

Think back to Chapter 14 Homeostasis: What cells in the islets of Langerhans release insulin and glucagon? How do insulin and glucagon regulate blood sugar level?

UNDERSTAND THESE TERMS

- endocrine gland
- endocrine system

15.2 Nervous communication

1 Copy and complete the table to show what happens on the neurone surface membrane during different events.

	Sodium–potassium pumps	Voltage-gated sodium channels	Voltage-gated potassium channels	Movement of sodium ions	Movement of potassium ions	Potential difference / mV
Resting potential						
Depolarisation						
Repolarisation						
Refractory period						

2   Figure 15.1 is a diagram of a cholinergic synapse.

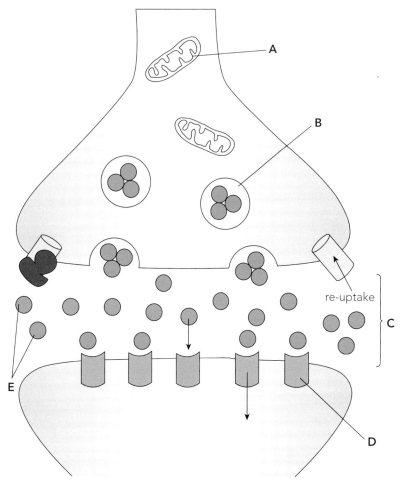

Figure 15.1

a   Identify structures **C**, **D** and **E**.   [3]

b   Describe the effects of an action potential arriving at the presynaptic
    neurone and how it affects structure **B**.   [5]

c   Structure **E** is processed and broken down by an enzyme in the
    postsynaptic membrane.
    Name the enzyme.   [1]

d   Structure **A** is essential in ensuring the synapse can receive another
    action potential. Suggest how its function allows it to do so.   [4]

                                                                        [Total: 13]

3 The Pacinian corpuscle is a pressure-sensitive receptor. It wraps around the nerve ending of a sensory neurone, with stretch-mediated sodium ion channels at the nerve ending, as shown in Figure 15.2.

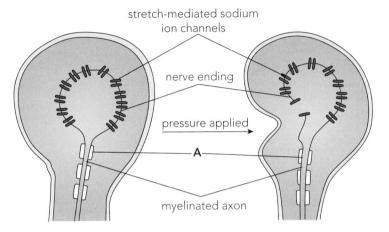

Figure 15.2

UNDERSTAND
THESE TERMS

*   depolarisation
*   repolarisation
*   refractory period
*   saltatory conduction
*   synapse

a   The stretch-mediated sodium ion channels open when pressure is applied. Suggest how that would trigger and transmit an action potential along the axon.   [4]

b   Identify structure **A** and explain its importance in increasing the speed of nervous transmission.   [4]

c   Using Figure 15.2, describe one similarity and two differences between the structure of the Pacinian corpuscle and the chemoreceptor cell.   [3]

[Total: 11]

15.3 Muscle contraction

1   Figure 15.3 shows the structure of a muscle. Name the sections labelled **A–F**.

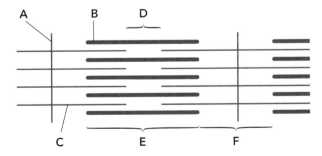

Figure 15.3: A diagram of a muscle

2   Figure 15.4 shows a part of a sarcomere undergoing muscle contraction.

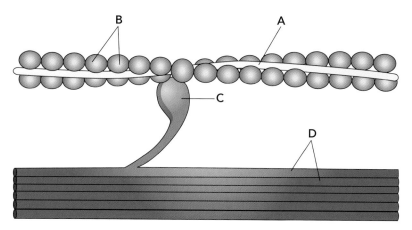

Figure 15.4

a   Structure **C** is currently attached to structure **A**.

  i   Identify structures **A**, **B** and **D**.   [3]

  ii   Describe how structure **C** can be detached from structure **A**.   [2]

b   Calcium ions are important in muscle contraction and in nervous
    transmission in synapses. Contrast the role and location of calcium ions
    in muscles and in synapses.   [8]

[Total: 13]

« RECALL AND CONNECT 2 «

Think back to Chapter 1 Cell structure: Eukaryotic cells have rough endoplasmic
reticulum (RER) and smooth endoplasmic reticulum (SER). The sarcoplasmic
reticulum is an example of SER. What is the difference in structure between
RER and SER? What are their functions?

**UNDERSTAND
THESE TERMS**

- sarcolemma
- sarcomere
- tropomyosin
- troponin

15.4 Control and coordination in plants

1   What are the functions of auxins, gibberellins and abscisic acid?

2   Outline how gibberellins cause seed germination.

3   The Venus fly trap is a carnivorous plant that uses electrical communication.

  a   Explain how the Venus fly trap detects a prey and traps it within its leaves. [5]

  b   Compare the effect of calcium ions in the Venus fly trap and in the
      synapse in humans.   [3]

[Total: 8]

4   Plants have hormones to coordinate their growth and responses.

    a   Contrast how hormones are produced and transported in animals and in plants. [4]

    b   Copy and complete the paragraph, using appropriate terms, to explain the mechanism of action for plant hormones.

Auxins, also known as IAA, are made in the .... of shoots and roots, where new cells are made and grown. They are chemicals that control cell growth by .... Auxins bind to cell surface receptors, which activates transport proteins to move .... ions into the cell wall. This in turn activates a protein called ...., which disrupts hydrogen bonds between .... microfibrils in the cell wall. Since the cell wall is less rigid, ... moves into the cell, expanding the cell, which leads to cell growth. [6]

[Total: 10]

> **UNDERSTAND THESE TERMS**
>
> - auxin
> - gibberellin
> - expansins
> - endosperm
> - aleurone layer

REFLECTION

How did you find the 'identify' questions in this chapter? Were you careful not to provide more responses than requested? How confident are you that you understand what is required from questions containing this command word?

SELF-ASSESSMENT CHECKLIST

Let's revisit the Knowledge focus and Exam skills focus for this chapter.

Decide how confident you are with each statement.

Now I can:	Show it	Needs more work	Almost there	Confident to move on
describe the features of the endocrine system with reference to the hormones insulin, glucagon and ADH	State the glands that produce insulin, glucagon and ADH, and describe how they travel to their target organs.			
compare the ways in which mammals coordinate responses to internal and external stimuli using the endocrine system and the nervous system	Contrast how the nervous system and the endocrine system work differently. Consider the speed at which signals are transmitted and how they are coordinated.			
describe the structure and function of sensory and motor neurones and outline how they function	Draw a labelled diagram for each type of neurone and state the direction of their nervous transmission.			
state the function of intermediate neurones	Describe where the intermediate neurones are found and what they do.			

CONTINUED

Now I can:	Show it	Needs more work	Almost there	Confident to move on
outline the roles of sensory receptor cells using a chemoreceptor cell in a human taste bud as an example	Draw a labelled diagram of a chemoreceptor cell and write a step-by-step description of how it works.			
describe and explain the transmission of nerve impulses	Write a step-by-step description of how resting potential is maintained, and how depolarisation and repolarisation occur.			
describe and explain the structure and function of cholinergic synapses	Draw a labelled diagram of a cholinergic synapse and write a step-by-step description of how it works.			
describe the ultrastructure of striated muscle and explain how muscles contract in response to impulses from motor neurones	Draw a flowchart or cycle diagram to show how the sliding filament model works to contract and relax a muscle. Include labelled diagrams to support your description.			
describe and explain the rapid response of the Venus fly trap	Draw a flowchart to show how the Venus fly trap can be triggered through nervous transmission.			
explain the role of auxin in elongation growth	Draw an annotated diagram to show how auxins promote shoot growth.			
describe the role of gibberellin in the germination of barley	Draw a flowchart to show how gibberellin triggers germination of seeds.			
answer more questions containing the 'identify' command word	Write your own 'identify' questions for different topics.			

Exam practice 6

This section contains past paper questions from previous Cambridge exams, which draw together your knowledge on a range of topics that you have covered up to this point. These questions give you the opportunity to test your knowledge and understanding. Additional past paper practice questions can be found in the accompanying digital material.

The following question has an example student response and commentary provided. Work through the question first, then compare your answer to the sample response and commentary. Are your answers different to the sample responses?

1   The enzyme alanine transaminase (ALT) is found in the liver. The function of ALT is to convert the amino acid α-ketoglutarate into another amino acid, glutamate.

    a   ALT can leak into the blood from liver tumour cells.

       An increase in the concentration of ALT in the blood causes a decrease in the water potential of the blood.

       State precisely the name **and** location of the cells where a change in the water potential of the blood would be detected. [1]

    b   Describe the homeostatic role of ADH when the water potential of the blood **decreases**. [5]

[Total: 6]

Cambridge International AS & A Level Biology (9700) Paper 42, Q1c,d, June 2020

Example student response	Commentary
1 a Osmoreceptors in the brain	While the student correctly named the cells that detect blood water potential, they did not give the precise location of the osmoreceptors in the brain, in the hypothalamus, as the question asked for. *This answer is awarded 0 out of 1 mark.*
b When the water potential of the blood decreases, this means the body is becoming dehydrated, so it needs to reabsorb more water from the filtrate. More ADH is released by the pituitary gland, which then travels through the bloodstream to the collecting duct of the kidneys. It binds to the cell surface receptors, which opens up more protein channels for water reabsorption.	The answer correctly included details of where ADH is released and how it targets the collecting duct by binding to its receptors on the cell surface membrane. However, it shows the student's misunderstanding of the actions of ADH. ADH does not open protein channels that are naturally found on the cell surface membrane, but it causes an enzyme cascade that moves vesicles with aquaporins to the cell surface to deposit the aquaporins for water reabsorption. In addition, the response should mention that water moves from the collecting duct into the blood by osmosis, which causes the water potential of the blood to rise. *This answer is awarded 2 out of 5 marks.*

Now attempt a similar question. Use the previous sample response and commentary to guide you as you answer.

2 Describe the effects of insulin on its main target tissues **and** explain how this leads to changes in blood glucose concentration. **[Total: 7]**

Cambridge International AS & A Level Biology (9700) Paper 41, Q10b, November 2018

The following question has an example student response and commentary provided. Work through the question first, then compare your answer to the sample response and commentary. Are your answers different to the sample responses? What information does this give you about your understanding of this topic?

3 Thyrotoxic myopathy (TM) is a neuromuscular disorder caused by overproduction of thyroid hormone thyroxine. One of the main symptoms of TM is muscle fatigue.

Fig. 3.1 outlines the effects of overproduction of thyroxine on striated muscle.

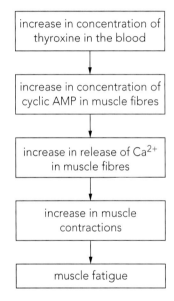

Fig. 3.1

a The concentration of thyroxine in the blood usually fluctuates around a set point.

Name the mechanism that keeps the concentration of thyroxine in the blood close to its set point. [1]

b Name the part of the striated muscle fibre that releases Ca^{2+}. [1]

c Describe the role of Ca^{2+}, troponin and tropomyosin in the contraction of striated muscle. [4]

[Total: 6]

Cambridge International AS & A Level Biology (9700) Paper 42, Q6a i–iii, June 2020

Example student response	Commentary
3 **a** Negative feedback	This answer and 'homeostasis' are both acceptable answers. *This answer is awarded 1 out of 1 mark.*
b Sarcoplasmic reticulum	The correct structure is identified. *This answer is awarded 1 out of 1 mark.*
c Ca^{2+} ions cause troponin and tropomyosin to both change shape and move on the actin, allowing myosin to bind with actin.	The student shows a basic understanding of how Ca^{2+} affects the shape of the proteins, but did not specify which protein Ca^{2+} binds to and how the change of shape of troponin affects the movement of tropomyosin. The answer also did not make clear how that movement allows actin to bind to myosin by exposing the binding sites on actin, which allow the myosin heads to attach to the binding sites. The response should also include that the movement or tilt of the myosin head pulls actin, contracting the striated muscle. *This answer is awarded 2 out of 4 marks.*

Now attempt an additional question on a similar topic. Use your previous answers, the sample responses and commentaries to guide you as you answer.

4 The Venus fly trap, *Dionaea muscipula*, is a carnivorous plant, native to wetlands of the East Coast of the USA. Mineral ions from decayed organisms are often washed away in these wetlands.

Fig. 4.1 shows a Venus fly trap leaf.

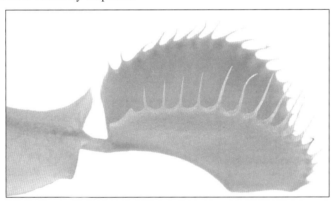

Fig. 4.1

a Suggest why a Venus fly trap benefits from catching insects in these wetlands. [2]

b **i** The leaves of the Venus fly trap will close if stimulated by an insect.

State which part of the leaf detects the stimulus. [1]

ii Explain how the plant does not waste energy by closing when it does not need to, such as when a large drop of rain touches the receptor. [1]

c   Fig. 4.2 is a graph of an action potential in a human neurone.

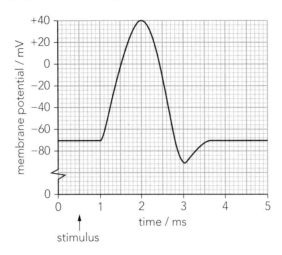

Fig. 4.2

Fig. 4.3 is a graph of an action potential in leaf cells of a Venus fly trap.

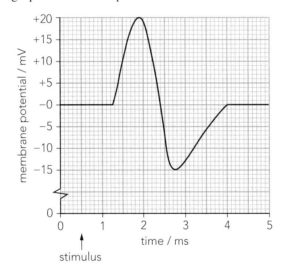

Fig. 4.3

With reference to Fig. 4.2 **and** Fig. 4.3, describe how the action potential of the Venus fly trap differs from that of a human.   [3]

d   Describe how the production of action potentials in the leaf cells of the Venus fly trap can result in the leaves closing and trapping an insect.   [5]

[Total: 12]

Cambridge International AS & A Level Biology (9700) Paper 42, Q7, November 2019

16 Inheritance

KNOWLEDGE FOCUS

In this chapter you will answer questions on:

- gametes and reproduction
- the production of genetic variation
- genetics
- monohybrid inheritance and genetic diagrams
- dihybrid inheritance
- the chi-squared (χ^2) test
- genes, proteins and phenotype
- control of gene expression.

EXAM SKILLS FOCUS

In this chapter you will:

- use higher-order thinking skills to answer a question using the command word 'suggest'.

Some questions require higher-order thinking skills such as judgement and critical thinking, and usually carry higher marks. The command word 'suggest' is an example of this.

Suggest	apply knowledge and understanding to situations where there are a range of valid responses in order to make proposals / put forward considerations

When you answer the 'suggest' question in this chapter, think about what the question is asking, what information is provided, and how to structure your response.

Synoptic questions often require you to use higher-order thinking skills.
You have explored synoptic questions in previous chapters.

16.1 Gametes and reproduction

1 What is the significance of reduction division in meiosis?

2 What is the difference between gametes, zygotes and embryos?

3 Meiosis consists of many stages.

   a State the stage(s) in meiosis where the following events take place.

     i Independent assortment occurs [1]

     ii Crossing over occurs [1]

     iii Centromere splits [1]

     iv Nuclear envelope reforms [1]

   b Lions, *Panthera leo*, have 38 chromosomes in their body cells.

     i Copy and complete the table to compare mitosis and meiosis in lions. [3]

	Mitosis	Meiosis
Number of divisions		
Number of chromosomes in daughter cells		
Number of daughter cells		

     ii Ligers are a hybrid species made from cross-breeding a male lion and a female tiger.

     Suggest why ligers are successfully produced despite lions and tigers being different species. [3]

[Total: 10]

REFLECTION

How did you find the 'suggest' question in this section? What higher-order thinking skills did you need to use to answer this question?

《 RECALL AND CONNECT 1 《

Think back to Chapter 5 The mitotic cell cycle: What is the purpose of mitosis? What occurs in each of the four stages in mitosis?

16.2 The production of genetic variation

1   What are some events that could lead to an increase in genetic variation?

2   What is the difference between 'gene' and 'allele'?

3   Explain how each of the following causes genetic variation to arise.

    a   Crossing over   [4]

    b   Independent assortment   [2]

    c   Fertilisation   [2]

[Total: 8]

UNDERSTAND THESE TERMS
- locus (plural: loci)
- allele
- independent assortment

16.3 Genetics

1   Assuming a gene has one dominant allele and one recessive allele. What are the three possible genotypes?

2   The petal colour gene C for a flower has two alleles – red allele C^R and white allele C^W. This gene exhibits codominance. The heterozygote outcome is blend of the two alleles. What are the possible genotypes and phenotypes for this flower?

3   Blood groups are determined by three alleles. Alleles I^A and I^B are codominant, whereas allele I^O is recessive to the other two.

    a   Explain what is meant by 'codominance'.   [1]

    b   For each of the following blood types, state the possible genotype(s).

      i   Type **A** blood   [1]

      ii   Type **B** blood   [1]

      iii   Type **O** blood   [1]

    c   With reference to the blood group system, explain the following terms.

      i   Phenotype   [2]

      ii   Multiple alleles   [2]

    d   A student suggested that in a cross between an individual with type **AB** blood and another with type **O** blood, their offspring could only have type **AB** blood and never type **O** blood.

    Use the information provided to explain the student's statement.   [6]

[Total: 14]

UNDERSTAND THESE TERMS
- genotype
- homozygous
- heterozygous
- phenotype

16.4 Monohybrid inheritance and genetic diagrams

1 What is the difference between:

   a F_1 generation and F_2 generation

   b genetic diagrams and Punnett squares?

2 Colour blindness is determined by a sex-linked gene. Its dominant allele **B** codes for normal vision, whereas the recessive allele **b** codes for colour blindness.

   a What are the possible genotypes and phenotypes for males?

   b What are the possible genotypes and phenotypes for females?

   c Which gender has a higher probability of having colour blindness? Use your answers to **a** and **b** to explain your choice.

3 Duchenne muscular dystrophy (DMD) is a recessive sex-linked condition in which children show progressive muscle degeneration. It can affect skeletal and cardiac muscles, causing physical weakness and heart problems, which reduces their life expectancy to 20–30 years.

   a Explain what is meant by a 'recessive sex-linked condition'. [2]

   b Using the letters Dd as the alleles for DMD:

     i Copy and complete the genetic diagram below to show the expected genotypes and phenotypes of the offspring from a cross between a healthy male and a carrier female. [4]

       Parental phenotype: Healthy male × Carrier female

       Parental genotype: .... × ....

       Gamete genotype(s): .... × ....

       Possible offspring genotype: ....

       Possible offspring phenotype: ....

     ii State the probability of an offspring with DMD being born from this cross. [1]

[Total: 7]

> **UNDERSTAND THESE TERMS**
> - codominant
> - Punnett square
> - F_1 generation
> - F_2 generation

16.5 Dihybrid inheritance

1   A plant species has a gene coding for its petal colours and another gene coding for its height. The dominant allele **R** codes for red petals, whereas the recessive allele **r** codes for white petals. The dominant allele **T** codes for a tall plant, whereas the recessive allele **t** codes for a dwarf plant.

Copy and complete the table to show the phenotype shown by each individual and the possible gamete genotypes that they can produce.

Genotype	Phenotype	Possible genotypes of gametes
RrTt		
RRTt		
rrTt		
rrtt		

2   Pigeons are birds that can have different feather colours and the distribution of the colour can vary in different parts of the body. This is based on the production of the colour pigment and where that pigment is placed. The allele that codes for brown feathers **B** is dominant to the allele coding for red feathers **b**. The other gene **G/g** codes for the distribution of the pigment. A full body deposition is coded by the dominant allele **G**, whereas partial deposition is coded by the recessive allele **g**, which results in the pigeon having brown or red patches on white feathers.

a   Deduce all possible genotype(s) for the following pigeons.

    i   Full body red feathers   [1]

    ii   White feathers with brown feather patches   [1]

    iii Full body brown feathers   [1]

b   Copy and complete the genetic diagram below to show the cross between a heterozygous pigeon with a pigeon with red feather patches. State the possible phenotypes of their offspring and include the probability of each phenotype in their offspring.   [5]

    Parental phenotype: brown × red feather patches
    Type of parental genotype: heterozygous × homozygous recessive
    Parental genotype: .... × ....
    Gamete genotype(s):   .... × ....
    Possible offspring genotype: ....
    Possible offspring phenotype: ....
    Probability: ....

c   The feather colour pigment is made through the conversion of a precursor protein. An enzyme is needed to catalyse this conversion. This enzyme is coded by the dominant version of the gene **I/i**.

    i   State the relationship between gene **I/i** and genes **B/b** and **G/g**.   [1]

    ii   State the phenotype of a pigeon with the genotype **ii**.   [1]

[Total: 10]

> **UNDERSTAND THESE TERMS**
> - carrier
> - dihybrid inheritance
> - epistasis
> - autosomal linkage
> - recombinant

16.6 The chi-squared (χ^2) test

1 What is the null hypothesis in a χ^2 test?

2 There are a few things to consider when doing a χ^2 test:

    a What does 'O' mean in the equation?

    b What does 'E' mean in the equation?

    c What does 'Σ' mean?

    d How do you find the degree of freedom?

    e Which probability value do we use?

    f If the χ^2 value is lower than the critical value, do we accept or reject the null hypothesis?

3 Potato plants vary in flower colours and stem height. These two traits are controlled by two genes **Rr** and **Hh**.

The allele for purple flowers (**R**) is dominant to the allele for white flowers (**r**).

The allele for tall stems (**H**) is dominant to the allele for shorter stems (**h**).

A scientist crosses a heterozygous potato plant with a homozygous recessive potato plant. The table shows the resulting offspring phenotypes.

Purple flowers + tall stems	Purple flowers + short stems	White flowers + tall stems	White flowers + short stems
34	17	18	31

> **UNDERSTAND THIS TERM**
>
> • chi-squared (χ^2) test

The scientist then did a χ^2 test to determine whether there is significant difference between the expected results with the observed outcome.

    a Determine the null hypothesis for this cross.   [1]

    b Copy and complete the table to calculate the χ^2 value.   [3]

Phenotype	Observed number (O)	Expected ratio	Expected number (E)	$O - E$	$(O - E)^2$	$(O - E)^2/E$
Purple flowers + tall stems						
Purple flowers + short stems						
White flowers + tall stems						
White flowers + short stems						
$\chi^2 = \Sigma \dfrac{(O - E)^2}{E}$						

[Total: 4]

16.7 Genes, proteins and phenotype

1   Copy and complete the table to summarise how these genes affect protein production and phenotype.

Gene	'Faulty' allele	Effect caused by 'faulty' allele	Condition caused
TYR			
HBB			
F8			
HTT			
Le			

2   Using examples from question **1**, explain how gene mutations could lead to a change in phenotype.   **[Total: 8]**

≪ RECALL AND CONNECT 2 ≪

Think back to Chapter 2 Biological molecules: What is the function of haemoglobin? How is the structure of haemoglobin adapted for its function?

16.8 Control of gene expression

1   Prokaryotes have the *lac* operon to control the production of lactase.

   a   Describe an 'operon'.

   b   What are the three structural genes in the *lac* operon?

   c   What is the function of the regulatory gene?

   d   When there is no lactose present, what happens at the operator?

   e   What happens when lactose is present?

2   The *lac* operon shown in Figure 16.1 is an example of how gene expression is controlled in prokaryotes.

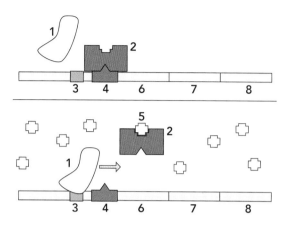

Figure 16.1

a   Use the numbers in Figure 16.1 to identify each component in the table.   [4]
    You may use the numbers once, more than once or not at all.

Name of component	Number
Structural genes	
Regulatory genes	
Proteins	
Carbohydrates	

b   State the function of components **6**, **7** and **8**.   [1]

c   Explain why components **1** and **2** cannot both bind to components **3** and **4** at the same time.   [2]

d   Explain the importance of this system of gene expression regulation in prokaryotes.   [2]

e   Using an example, describe how eukaryotes control gene expression differently from prokaryotes.   [5]

[Total: 14]

> **UNDERSTAND THESE TERMS**
>
> - structural gene
> - regulatory gene
> - inducible enzyme
> - repressible enzyme
> - transcription factor

REFLECTION

Lots of exam questions test you on your ability to link various concepts together, then apply them in an unfamiliar context (for example, on a disease or condition that you have not come across before). How could you best prepare yourself in learning the links between concepts? Once you have identified those links, how do you assess whether you remember the details and understand the connections properly?

If you have identified an area that you are unsure of, what should you do to reinforce your learning on that area?

SELF-ASSESSMENT CHECKLIST

Let's revisit the Knowledge focus and Exam skills focus for this chapter.

Decide how confident you are with each statement.

Now I can:	Show it	Needs more work	Almost there	Confident to move on
describe the process of meiosis, and explain its significance in terms of maintaining chromosome number in sexual reproduction and producing genetically different offspring	Draw a diagram flowchart to show what occurs in the cell throughout meiosis.			
describe and explain how different alleles of genes affect phenotype	Give examples of conditions that show dominant and recessive phenotype depending on their alleles.			
construct and interpret genetic diagrams showing monohybrid crosses, including the involvement of dominant, recessive and codominant alleles and sex linkage	Pick an example of monohybrid inheritance in the coursebook, then draw a genetic diagram to show parental phenotype, parental genotype, gamete genotype, Punnett square of the cross, offspring genotype and phenotype.			
construct and interpret genetic diagrams showing dihybrid crosses, including the involvement of dominant, recessive and codominant alleles, autosomal linkage and epistasis	Pick an example of dihybrid inheritance in the coursebook, then draw a genetic diagram to show parental phenotype, parental genotype, gamete genotype, Punnett square of the cross, offspring genotype and phenotype. Describe what autosomal linkage and epistasis are.			
use the chi-squared test to determine the significance of differences between observed and expected results in genetic crosses	Write down the null hypothesis of the chi-squared test. Write down the equation and state what each part of the equation represents.			

CONTINUED

Now I can:	Show it	Needs more work	Almost there	Confident to move on
explain the relationship between genes, proteins and phenotype, using the genes *TYR*, *HBB*, *F8* and *HTT* as examples	Construct a table to summarise the effect and condition caused by each gene mutation.			
explain how the alleles **Le** and **le** control gibberellin production and hence stem elongation	Draw a flowchart to show the effects on the plant if it has **LeLe**, **Lele** or **lele.**			
use the *lac* operon to explain how gene expression is controlled in prokaryotes	Draw an annotated diagram of the *lac* operon and explain the functions of each component, including the repressor and RNA polymerase.			
describe how transcription factors are involved in the control of gene expression in eukaryotes, including the role of gibberellin and DELLA protein repressor in plants	Draw a flowchart to illustrate how gibberellins interact with DELLA proteins.			
use higher-order thinking skills to answer a question using the command word 'suggest'	Explain to a friend what the command word 'suggest' means and answer a 'suggest' question.			

17 Selection and evolution

KNOWLEDGE FOCUS

In this chapter you will answer questions on:

- variation
- natural selection
- genetic drift and the founder effect
- the Hardy–Weinberg principle
- artificial selection
- evolution
- identifying evolutionary relationships.

EXAM SKILLS FOCUS

In this chapter you will:

- practise planning your response before writing answers to long-form questions.

In Chapter 14, you looked at how to plan your response before answering long-form questions. You will revisit this in this chapter and will practise more questions to improve your answers. Make sure you go back to Chapter 14 to refresh your memory on how to plan responses.

17.1 Variation

1 What are potential causes of genetic variation?

2 What is the difference between continuous and discontinuous variation?

3 A student investigates variation in a population of chickens, specifically their weight and feather colour.

Match each of the following 10 statements to the aspect it applies to. Some statements may apply to both aspects.

Weight:

Feather colour:

1	Presented with a bar chart	6	Presented with a histogram
2	May be affected by environment	7	May be a result of epistasis
3	May be controlled by genes with additive effects	8	May be controlled by polygenes
4	Is a discontinuous variation	9	Is a continuous variation
5	Can be measured quantitatively	10	Can be measured qualitatively

[Total: 11]

> **UNDERSTAND THESE TERMS**
> - genetic variation
> - phenotypic variation
> - discontinuous variation
> - continuous variation
> - polygenes

17.2 Natural selection

1 These statements describe different types of selection.
Decide which of the three selection types shown in the table each statement describes.

Some statements may apply to more than one type of selection.

A There is a change in allele frequency in the population.
B There is no change in the environment.
C This selection maintains polymorphism in a population.
D There is at least one selection pressure in the environment.
E This is where the two extreme phenotypes are favoured for survival.
F This is where the most common phenotype is favoured for survival.
G This is where one phenotype is favoured for survival.

Stabilising selection	Directional selection	Disruptive selection

> **UNDERSTAND THESE TERMS**
> - selection pressure
> - stabilising selection
> - directional selection
> - disruptive selection
> - polymorphism

2   Put the following statements in the correct order to describe how natural selection takes place.

A   The favourable allele is passed onto offspring.

B   More individuals in the population have the favourable adaptations to survive in the new selection pressure.

C   Mutations occur, leading to pre-existing variation in a population.

D   Over time, the frequency of the favourable allele increases.

E   Some individuals are well adapted to the change in environment and are more likely to survive and reproduce.

F   There is a change in selection pressure.

3   Penicillin is a type of β-lactam antibiotic that can be prescribed to people with bacterial infections.

β-lactamase is an enzyme released by bacteria that destroys the structure of β-lactam antibiotics.

a   Figure 17.1 shows how the number of β-lactamase enzymes that are identified by scientists has changed over time, since the first β-lactam antibiotic was used.

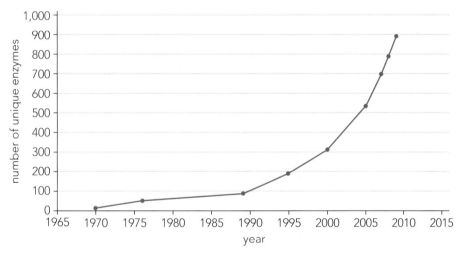

Figure 17.1

i   Using Figure 17.1, calculate the rate per year of unique β-lactamase identified from the years 2000 to 2010.

Show your working.   [2]

ii   Suggest a reason for the trend shown in Figure 17.1.   [4]

b To prevent β-lactamase from destroying β-lactam antibiotics, a β-lactamase inhibitor called clavulanic acid shown in Figure 17.2 is often prescribed alongside the antibiotic.

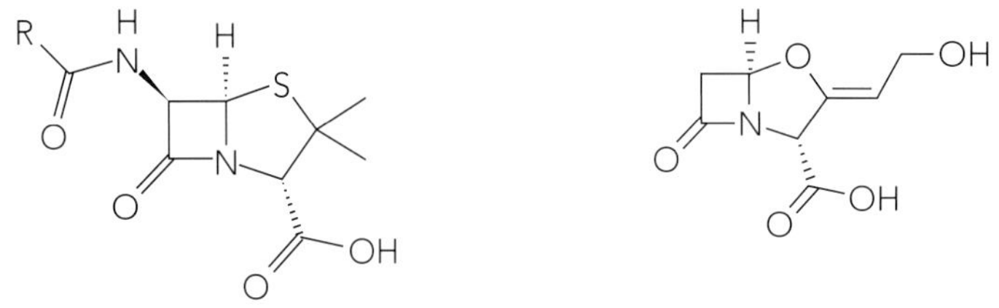

penicillin   clavulanic acid

Figure 17.2

Using Figure 17.2, suggest how clavulanic acid is able to inhibit β-lactamase enzymes released by bacteria. [4]

c Penicillin was first isolated from the fungus *Penicillium rubens*. However, due to extensive use, most bacteria developed resistance against it. Most penicillins used currently are made by a different species *Penicillium chrysogenum*.

Explain how bacteria developed resistance against the penicillin from *P. rubens*. [6]

[Total: 16]

≪ RECALL AND CONNECT 1 ≪

Think back to Chapter 3 Enzymes: Describe the difference in mechanism between competitive and non-competitive inhibition.

17.3 Genetic drift and the founder effect

1 Which genetic phenomenon can be caused by each scenario?

   a A few individuals moving away from their original population and repopulating elsewhere.

   b A catastrophic event killing most of the population, with a few survivors remaining.

   c Plant seeds landing on different types of soil, where only those on fertile soil germinated.

2 What is the effect of genetic drift and the founder effect on the size of the gene pool?

3 Explain some potential causes and effects of a reduction in the gene pool. **[Total: 8]**

UNDERSTAND THESE TERMS
• genetic drift
• gene pool
• founder effect
• evolutionary bottleneck

17.4 The Hardy–Weinberg principle

1   What does each of the following parts of the Hardy–Weinberg equations mean?

   a p

   b p^2

   c q

   d q^2

   e $2pq$

2   State three assumptions that are made when using the Hardy–Weinberg principle.

3   Cystic fibrosis is a genetic condition where there is a build-up of mucus in the body, especially the trachea and bronchi in the respiratory system. It is caused by the recessive allele of the gene *CFTR*.

There are currently 10 834 people in the UK with cystic fibrosis.
There are approximately 68 000 000 people in the UK.

   a   State the function of mucus in the trachea and bronchi.   [1]

   b   Give the names of the two types of cell that release mucus.   [2]

   c   The Hardy–Weinberg equations can be used to estimate allele frequency within a population:

$p + q = 1$

$p^2 + 2pq + q^2 = 1$

     i   Use the Hardy–Weinberg equations to calculate the percentage of people in the UK that are carriers of cystic fibrosis.

       Give your answer to two decimal places.

       Show your working.   [3]

     ii   The Hardy–Weinberg principle does not give an accurate estimation of the percentage of cystic fibrosis carriers in the UK due to fluctuations in the population.

       Suggest two other reasons why the Hardy–Weinberg principle may not be suitable for estimating allele frequency for cystic fibrosis in the UK.   [2]

[Total: 8]

17.5 Artificial selection

1 Which of the statements 1, 2, 3 and 4 describe artificial selection and which ones describe natural selection?

1	Offspring are well adapted to the selection pressures in the environment
2	Offspring may have homozygosity
3	Offspring have specific traits chosen by humans
4	There is variation among the resulting offspring

2 Give one example of artificial selection in animals and one in plants.

3 Describe how artificial selection is carried out and assess its use in agriculture, using examples.

[Total: 12]

UNDERSTAND THESE TERMS

- artificial selection
- inbreeding depression
- inbreeding
- outbreeding
- hybrid vigour

REFLECTION

Tackling long-form questions can be daunting at times, but they are not as difficult as they appear once you notice some key words in the question. Remind yourself of what different command words mean, for example, what is the difference between 'describe' and 'explain'? What sort of information should be included in an 'explain' question? How can the number of marks allocated to each long-form question help you plan your answers?

17.6 Evolution

1 List at least three reasons for a population of the same species to go through reproductive isolation.

2 What is the difference between allopatric and sympatric speciation?

3 Charles Darwin studied finches during his time in the Galapagos archipelago, which is a group of closely scattered islands in the Pacific Ocean. He initially thought that the birds were unrelated to each other, until another scientist named John Gould informed him that the birds originated from the same group of finches but then formed 12 new species. Figure 17.3 shows the illustration of the beaks of four Galapagos finches, found in the second edition of *Journal of Researches* written by Darwin in 1845.

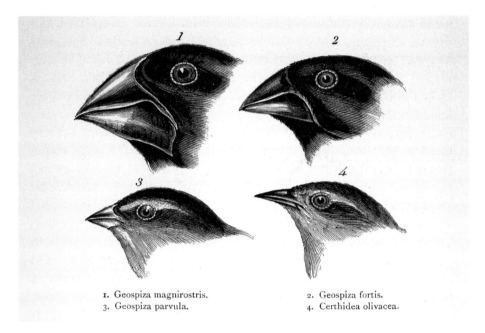

1. Geospiza magnirostris.
2. Geospiza fortis.
3. Geospiza parvula.
4. Certhidea olivacea.

Figure 17.3

a   Using Figure 17.3, suggest why Darwin thought the birds were
of different species.   [1]

b   The four species of finches shown in Figure 17.3 were found on different
islands in the Galapagos.

   i   State the type of speciation observed in Darwin's finches.   [1]

   ii Suggest how the finches developed different characteristics despite
having originated from the same species.   [5]

[Total: 7]

**UNDERSTAND
THESE TERMS**

- reproductive isolation
- allopatric speciation
- sympatric speciation
- ecological separation
- behavioural separation

17.7 Identifying evolutionary relationships

1   How can DNA sequences be used to determine the evolutionary relationship
between different species?

2   Which three organelles contain DNA in eukaryotic cells?

3   Cytochrome c is a protein that is involved in the electron transport chain in
aerobic respiration. Its DNA sequence is highly conserved across eukaryotic
species, therefore it is often used in the study of evolutionary biology.

a   State the exact location of cytochrome c in a cell.   [1]

b   Explain why the DNA sequence of cytochrome c would be highly
conserved across species.   [6]

c   A section of the DNA sequence for cytochrome *c* found in different species is listed in the table.

Organism	DNA sequence
Ancestor cell	A T T A G C G A C C A G T A T A T C
A	C T A A T C C C C C G T T T A T C
B	C T T A T C G A C C C G T T T A T C
C	A T T A G C G A C C A G T T T A T C
D	T T A A T C C C C C C G T T A A T C

i   These differences in DNA sequence are a result of mutation.

State which type of mutation is shown in the sequences in the table. Explain why such mutation is allowed to be passed on.   [3]

ii Using the information provided, deduce the order in time at which each organism has diverged from its common ancestor.   [3]

Ancestor → .... → .... → .... → ....

[Total: 13]

≪ RECALL AND CONNECT 2 ≪

Think back to Chapter 6 Nucleic acids and protein synthesis: Remember especially the amino acid sequence and the importance of its degenerate nature. What are the three components that make up a DNA nucleotide? How is a DNA nucleotide different from an RNA nucleotide? The genetic code is described as 'degenerate'. What does this mean? Explain its importance.

REFLECTION

Sometimes, exam questions may have an unfamiliar context. For example, the question may be based on a new organism or condition that you have not come across before. Remember, you will never be asked questions about topics that are not included in the syllabus. How can you best approach this type of question? What can you do to interpret and extract information from the question? How do you decide what sort of knowledge the question wants you to use?

SELF-ASSESSMENT CHECKLIST

Let's revisit the Knowledge focus and Exam skills focus for this chapter.

Decide how confident you are with each statement.

Now I can:	Show it	Needs more work	Almost there	Confident to move on
explain that genetic and environmental factors affect phenotypic variation	List the genetic and environmental factors that can affect the phenotype of an organism.			
explain the differences between continuous and discontinuous variation	Draw a table to list the differences between continuous and discontinuous variation.			
explain how natural selection takes place, including reference to the development of antibiotic resistance in bacteria	Write down how bacteria develop antibiotic resistance using numbered steps.			
explain the differences between stabilising, disruptive and directional selection	Draw three graphs to show the genotype frequency shown in stabilising, disruptive and directional selection.			
explain how the founder effect and genetic drift may affect allele frequencies	Draw diagrams to show how the founder effect and genetic drift may occur, resulting in changes in allele frequency.			
use the Hardy–Weinberg equations	Write down the two Hardy–Weinberg equations and what the letters mean.			
describe the principles of selective breeding, including examples	Write down how selective breeding is carried out in numbered steps.			
outline the theory of evolution in terms of changes to gene pools	Write down how a species evolves to become a different species by natural selection. Write in numbered steps.			
discuss the use of DNA sequencing to determine relationships between species	State how similarities in DNA sequences inform us of evolutionary relationships between species.			

CONTINUED

Now I can:	Show it	Needs more work	Almost there	Confident to move on
explain how new species can be formed by allopatric and sympatric processes	Draw two diagrams to show how allopatric and sympatric speciation occur.			
plan my response before writing answers to long-form questions	Read and annotate an exam skills question to see what it is asking of you. Then list key words or concepts that you should include in your final answer.			

Exam practice 7

This section contains past paper questions from previous Cambridge exams, which draw together your knowledge on a range of topics that you have covered up to this point. These questions give you the opportunity to test your knowledge and understanding. Additional past paper practice questions can be found in the accompanying digital material.

The following question has an example student response and commentary provided. Work through the question first, then compare your answer to the sample response and commentary. Are your answers different to the sample responses?

1   Flower colour is important in sexual reproduction of insect-pollinated plants.

In the rosy periwinkle, *Catharanthus roseus*, flower colour is controlled by three genes, **R/r**, **D/d** and **P/p**, which interact together to control flower colour.

Fig. 1.1 is a drawing of a rosy periwinkle.

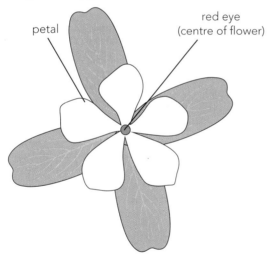

petal

red eye
(centre of flower)

Fig. 1.1

The presence of the **R** allele results in a red pigment in the centre of the flower (red eye).

The **D** allele and the **P** allele are only expressed when the **R** allele is present.

*   When the **D** allele and the **R** allele are present, the flower has dark pink petals with a red eye.

*   When the **P** allele and the **R** allele are present, the flower has pale pink petals with a red eye.

*   When the **D** allele, the **P** allele and the **R** allele are all present, the flower has dark pink petals with a red eye.

*   The recessive alleles **r**, **d** and **p** result in no pigments being produced and the flower has white petals and no red eye.

a Deduce the phenotypes of these rosy periwinkle genotypes. [4]

RR dd PP ....

Rr Dd Pp ....

rr Dd Pp ....

RR dd pp ....

b The pigments causing flower colour in the rosy periwinkle are formed by a biosynthetic pathway.

The **R** allele mutated to produce the **r** allele.

The **r** allele codes for a non-functional protein.

Explain how the mutation that changes **R** to **r** results in no red pigment being synthesised in the flower of rosy periwinkle. [4]

c One mutation that changes the flower colour of rosy periwinkle occurs in a region of the DNA that does not code for a polypeptide.

Suggest what function this region of DNA might perform. [1]

[Total: 9]

Cambridge International AS & A Level Biology (9700) Paper 42, Q4b, November 2019

Example student response	Commentary
1 **a** **RR dd PP**: red eye + pale pink petals **Rr Dd Pp**: red eye + dark pink petals **rr Dd Pp**: no red eye + dark pink petals **RR dd pp**: red eye + white petals	The question says that alleles **D/d** and **P/p** can only be expressed if there is the dominant allele **D**. Therefore, the third answer for **rr Dd Pp** is incorrect, the answer should be no red eye + white petals. *This answer is awarded 3 out of 4 marks.*
b The **R** allele codes for the red pigment to be formed. If the mutation occurs, then the pigment produced will be white instead, resulting in no red eye.	Notice the question is asking the student to *explain how* the mutation causes this phenotype. It also mentioned that the pigments are formed through a biosynthetic pathway, not directly coded by the gene **R/r**. A good answer should suggest what kind of mutation may cause an effect on protein production. It should also refer to how a protein may become non-functional, based on one's knowledge of protein structure. *This answer is awarded 0 out of 4 marks.*
c It may regulate gene expression.	The response correctly identifies that the region of DNA may control the expression of the flower colour. *This answer is awarded 1 out of 1 mark.*

2 Now that you've gone through the commentary, attempt writing a mark scheme for question **1b**. This will check that you've understood exactly why each mark has (or has not) been allocated. The more often you do this, and the better you get to know the way mark schemes are written, the more confident you will feel about your answers in an exam.

The following question has an example student response and commentary provided. Work through the question first, then compare your answer to the sample response and commentary. Are your answers different to the sample responses? What information does this give you about your understanding of this topic?

3 The stickleback fish, *Gasterosteus aculeatus*, has two distinct forms, the saltwater form and the freshwater form. The larger, freshwater form is thought to have evolved from the smaller, saltwater form. Both forms have armour plating on each side of the body. The plates are made of bone and contain a high proportion of calcium.

The ectodysplasin gene, *EDA*, codes for a protein involved in the development of armour plates. The *EDA* gene has two alleles, low armour and high armour.

Three main morphs of armour plating have been described.

Complete morph armour plating:
- is found mainly in the saltwater form
- has many plates from head to tail to cover most of the body
- provides defence against large, predatory fish
- limits the growth of the fish.

Partial morph armour plating:
- is found mainly in the freshwater form
- has a reduced number of plates to cover only part of the body.

Low morph armour plating:
- is found mainly in the freshwater form
- has very few, undeveloped plates and no body cover.

a Explain why the variation in armour plating in stickleback fish can be described as discontinuous. [2]

b In 1982, at Loberg Lake in Southern Alaska, the entire freshwater stickleback fish population was accidentally destroyed by humans.

In 1990, a new population of stickleback fish was found in the lake. Most of these fish had armour plates from head to tail on each side.

Suggest why these new stickleback fish have armour plates from head to tail on each side, despite living in freshwater. [1]

c From 1990, annual sampling took place in the lake.

Each year showed a reduction in the number of individuals with complete morph armour plating (from head to tail on each side). This change took place in a relatively short period of time.

In 1990, 96% of the stickleback fish population had complete morph armour plating.

In 1993, 39% of the stickleback fish population had complete morph armour plating.

Explain how natural selection has occurred in this new stickleback fish population. [5]

[Total: 8]

Cambridge International AS & A Level Biology (9700) Paper 42, Q2, November 2019

Example student response	Commentary
3 **a** It is discontinuous variation as the characteristics are in distinct groups and not in numbers.	One mark is given for correctly identifying what discontinuous variation is. A second mark can be scored if the student expands on what may have caused discontinuous variation in the first place. *This answer is awarded 1 out of 2 marks.*
b Mutation occurred.	Other possible answers include reference to colonisation and the ability to defend themselves from predators. *This answer is awarded 1 out of 1 mark.*
c Since the complete armour limits the growth of fish, most have mutated to have less armour. They are able to survive under selection pressure and are favoured to reproduce. They pass on the favourable allele for less armour and over time more individuals and offspring have less armour.	Organisms are unable to mutate within their lifetime to gain new adaptations, so the first statement highlights a common misconception students have. Instead, it is pre-existing genetic variation that causes them to be different. There could be more details about why having less armour is a survival advantage and how the allele frequency has changed in the population. *This answer is awarded 3 out of 5 marks.*

Now you have read the commentary to the previous question, here is a similar question that you should attempt. Use the information from the previous response and commentary to guide you as you answer.

4 **a** In continuous variation, a population shows a range of phenotypes between two extremes with no distinct groups. Height and mass are examples of phenotypic traits that show continuous variation.

Describe the genetic basis for continuous variation. [3]

b Environmental factors can contribute to continuous variation.

Suggest **two** environmental factors that may affect the body mass of an animal. [2]

c Humans have used selective breeding (artificial selection) for thousands of years to improve the quality of livestock.

Outline the principles of selective breeding in livestock. [4]

[Total: 9]

Cambridge International AS & A Level Biology (9700) Paper 42, Q8, June 2021

Now attempt the following two questions that are on similar topics.

5   The black pigment melanin, which contributes to hair, skin and eye colour, is produced by cells known as melanocytes.

   a   In people with albinism, the melanocytes do not produce melanin. Albinism is caused by an inherited gene mutation.

      i   Outline how a gene mutation may occur.   [4]

      ii   Albinism is an autosomal recessive condition.

          Explain what is meant by the term *recessive*.   [1]

      iii   Using appropriate symbols, draw a genetic diagram to show how a man and a woman, who both produce melanin, could have a child with albinism.   [3]

   b   Melanin is produced by the action of the enzyme tyrosinase on the amino acid tyrosine.

      A study was carried out to investigate the effect of an extract of the starfish *Patiria pectinifera* on the activity of tyrosinase.

      Table 5.1 shows the results of this study.

concentration of starfish extract / µg cm^{-3}	percentage tyrosinase activity
0	100
4	90
8	77
16	68
32	56
64	46
128	32

Table 5.1

      Suggest how the starfish extract affects the activity of tyrosinase.   [3]

                                                                            [Total: 11]

Cambridge International AS & A Level Biology (9700) Paper 42, Q6, March 2018

6   a   Meiosis is one process that contributes to genetic variation.

      i   State **precisely** the stage of meiosis where single chromosomes line up on the equator.   [1]

      ii   Outline the events taking place during anaphase I of meiosis.   [2]

      iii   Describe how crossing over during meiosis leads to genetic variation.   [2]

b Mutation also causes genetic variation. Some populations of water hemp, *Amaranthus tuberculatus*, have evolved herbicide resistance as a result of a mutation. This is a problem for farmers as water hemp grows in crop fields, lowering productivity.

Two populations of water hemp were tested for resistance to the herbicide mesotrione. One was a population known to be resistant (control) and the other was a test population, whose resistance was unknown.

- Leaves were removed and immersed in a radioactively labelled solution of mesotrione.

- The leaves absorbed some mesotrione and became radioactive.

- Resistant leaves are able to degrade mesotrione by metabolism.

- The time for 50% of absorbed mesotrione to degrade was calculated by measuring the radioactivity of the leaves.

The results are shown in Table 6.1.

population of water hemp	mean time for 50% of absorbed mesotrione to degrade / hours	standard deviation
test	27.5	4.75
control	10.1	2.34

Table 6.1

i Explain how the results in Table 6.1 show that the two populations differ in their resistance to mesotrione. [2]

ii Explain why this example of genetic variation is important for natural selection in water hemp populations. [2]

iii Farmers can send in a sample of leaves of water hemp from their fields to a laboratory to be tested for resistance to mesotrione or other herbicides.

Suggest the benefit of this to a farmer. [1]

c The null hypothesis states there is no significant difference between the mean times for 50% of absorbed mesotrione to degrade in the two populations.

A *t*-test can be carried out to compare these two means.
The critical value for *t* at the $p = 0.05$ significance level is 2.23.

i Use the formula in Fig. 6.1 to calculate the value of *t*.
Show your working. [2]

$$t = \frac{|\bar{x}_1 - \bar{x}_2|}{\sqrt{\left(\frac{s_1^2}{n_1} + \frac{s_2^2}{n_2}\right)}}$$

Key

$\bar{x}$ = mean
s = standard deviation
n_1 = 6 (number of readings for test population)
n_2 = 6 (number of readings for test population)

Fig. 6.1

ii Use your calculated value of *t* to explain whether the null hypothesis should be accepted or rejected. [2]

[Total: 14]

Cambridge International AS & A Level Biology (9700) Paper 41, Q3, November 2018

18 Classification, biodiversity and conservation

KNOWLEDGE FOCUS

In this chapter you will answer questions on:

- classification
- biodiversity
- maintaining biodiversity
- protecting endangered species
- controlling alien species
- international conservation organisations.

EXAM SKILLS FOCUS

In this chapter you will:

- practise distinguishing core information from other instructional text.

Exam questions may include additional information to illustrate the context the questions are based on. This is often useful information that you may need to use within your answer. In this chapter, you will practise such question types and learn how to extract core information and use it in the right context to structure the answer.

18.1 Classification

1 List all taxonomic groups in the hierarchical classification system. Start from the highest to lowest.

2 What are the three domains and the four kingdoms?

3 What are the two aspects considered when classifying viruses?

4 Grizzly bears (Figure 18.1a) and polar bears (Figure 18.1b) are both members of the genus *Ursus*.

Figure 18.1a

Figure 18.1b

a Scientist A suggests that grizzly bears and polar bears should belong to the same species. Using the information provided, discuss their statement. [5]

b Polar bears and giant pandas (*Ailuropoda melanoleuca*) originated from a common ancestor.

Copy and complete the table for the classification of giant pandas. [6]

Domain	
Kingdom	
	Chordata
	Mammalia
	Carnivora
Genus	
Species	

[Total: 11]

5 All living organisms are grouped in a taxonomical classification system.

a The two domains Bacteria and Archaea used to belong to the same group called Prokaryota.

  i State one similarity between Bacteria and Archaea. [1]

  ii Give one reason why Bacteria and Archaea were separated into two domains. [1]

b There are four kingdoms that belong to the domain Eukarya.

Copy and complete the table to compare the four kingdoms. [4]

Kingdom	Animalia	Plantae	Fungi	Protoctista
Cell wall is present or absent?				
May contain chloroplasts				
Autotrophic				
Heterotrophic				

c Viruses do not belong to any of the domains. Explain how viruses are classified. [2]

[Total: 8]

≪ RECALL AND CONNECT 1 ≪

Think back to Chapter 1 Cell structure: What are the differences between eukaryotic and prokaryotic cell structure? Copy and complete the table to compare their cell structures.

Cell features	Prokaryotic cells	Eukaryotic cells
Size of ribosome		
Presence of membrane-bound organelles		
DNA structure		
Presence of nucleus		
Location of chromosomes		
Chemical in cell wall (if present)		

18.2 Biodiversity

1   What are the three main levels of biodiversity?

2   For each scenario **a** and **b**, which sampling method should be used?

    a   Find population of animals.

    b   Find the distribution of species across sand dunes.

3   A student wants to compare the biodiversity of plants in two areas within a park by measuring the abundance of different types of plants in those two areas. One of the plants in the area is clover leaf.

    Outline the process and equipment needed to measure the abundance of clovers in a 20 m × 20 m area.

    You do not need to include calculations.

[Total: 6]

UNDERSTAND THESE TERMS

- ecosystem
- community
- habitat
- niche
- Simpson's index of diversity (*D*)

4 *Hyacinthoides non-scripta*, also known as the common bluebell, is a plant that is found mainly in the British Isles and the western parts of Atlantic Europe. The common bluebell can grow in woodlands and open areas.

A group of students decided to investigate how light intensity and soil pH may affect the growth and distribution of the common bluebell.

a State the type of sampling and equipment that the students should use to find the distribution of common bluebells. [2]

b The students measure the number of common bluebells and soil pH along an area. Their findings are recorded in a table.

   i State the null hypothesis in their investigation. [1]

   ii Using the table and the equation provided, calculate the Spearman's rank correlation coefficient (r_s) between soil pH and the number of common bluebells. Copy and complete the table. The first column has been completed for you.

      Give your final answer to three decimal places. Show your working. [4]

Soil pH	Number of common bluebells	Rank of soil pH	Rank of number of common bluebells	D	D²
7	32	4.5			
4	76	1			
5	59	2			
6	53	3			
9	29	7			
8	32	6			
7	34	4.5			
				ΣD^2	

$$r_s = \left[1 - \frac{6\Sigma D^2}{N^3 - N}\right]$$

   iii Using your answer to **bii**, explain whether there is a correlation or not between soil pH and the number of common bluebells. [4]

   iv A student within the group said that they cannot be certain of their findings. Suggest what other data they can use to verify their conclusion. [2]

[Total: 13]

18.3 Maintaining biodiversity

1   List some potential causes of extinction.

2   What are some main reasons to maintain biodiversity?

3   The dodo, *Raphus cucullatus*, was an endemic species of flightless bird that was once native to the island of Mauritius in the Indian Ocean. They built their nests on the ground of forests and it is believed they typically laid one single egg at one time. They evolved in isolation and had never encountered humans until they were first discovered by Dutch sailors in the late 1500s. The sailors travelled there along with other animals, such as dogs and pigs, and built shelter on the island.

   However, soon after its discovery, the dodo became extinct in approximately 1700.

   a   Using the information provided, suggest how the dodo became extinct.   [6]

   b   Give three reasons why the sailors should have maintained biodiversity on the Mauritius island.   [3]

   [Total: 9]

18.4 Protecting endangered species

1   There are several ways that endangered species are protected. How does each method work to protect these organisms?

   a   National parks

   b   Zoos

   c   Assisted reproduction

   d   Frozen zoos and seed banks

2   Many zoos use assisted reproduction to conserve endangered species. This can be done through *in vitro* fertilisation (IVF).

   a   State one difference between artificial insemination and IVF.   [1]

   b   State the process by which cells in the zygote increase.   [1]

   c   The embryos may then be stored in a 'frozen zoo'.

   i   Explain what a 'frozen zoo' is and its significance.   [2]

   ii   Suggest one challenge that scientists face when freezing embryos.   [2]

   iii   Apart from a 'frozen zoo', describe one other way that the embryos may then be used soon after fertilisation and explain its importance.   [2]

   [Total: 8]

> UNDERSTAND THESE TERMS

- surrogacy
- *in vitro* fertilisation (IVF)
- seed bank

≪ RECALL AND CONNECT 2 ≪

Think back to Chapter 5 The mitotic cell cycle and Chapter 6 Nucleic acid and protein synthesis: Copy and complete the table to compare the two types of cell division in animals.

	Mitosis	Meiosis
Number of divisions		
Number of daughter cells produced		
Genetic content of daughter cells		
Formation of bivalent?		
Purpose		
Where does this occur in the body?		

18.5 Controlling alien species

1   Explain what is meant by an 'alien species' and outline its negative impacts on an ecosystem.   [Total: 4]

UNDERSTAND THIS TERM

• alien species

18.6 International conservation organisations

1   What is the main aim of:

   a   the International Union for Conservation of Nature (IUCN)?

   b   the Convention on International Trade in Endangered Species of Wild Fauna and Flora (CITES)?

2   Conservation biology is the study of methods and practices that are observed to protect and restore biodiversity.

   a   Explain what the three types of biodiversity are.   [3]

   b   State three reasons for protecting and restoring biodiversity.   [3]

                                                                        [Total: 6]

REFLECTION

How did you find the exam skills questions, especially the ones that provided lots of background information and context? Did you find it easy to extract core information from the texts provided and use it in the right context? Check your answers and see if you were able to do so. If you did, how did you identify key information when reading the question? If not, can you think of ways that could help you with this?

SELF-ASSESSMENT CHECKLIST

Let's revisit the Knowledge focus and Exam skills focus for this chapter.

Decide how confident you are with each statement.

Now I can:	Show it	Needs more work	Almost there	Confident to move on
discuss the meaning of the term 'species' and explain how species are classified	State the three species concepts and describe what they mean.			
outline the characteristic features of the three domains and of the four kingdoms of eukaryotic organisms	Make a table to compare the features of the three domains and repeat for the four kingdoms.			
outline how viruses are classified	State the two ways that viruses are classified.			
explain the importance of biodiversity in terms of ecosystems, habitats, species and the genetic diversity within each species	Describe what is meant by the different types of biodiversity.			
investigate ecosystems using techniques for assessing the occurrence, abundance and distribution of species	Make a list of equipment needed for different methods of sampling animals and plants.			
explain how species may become extinct	List the causes of extinction.			
calculate Simpson's index of diversity and use it to compare the biodiversity of different areas	Describe what a high and a low Simpson's index indicate about the biodiversity of an area.			
use statistical methods to analyse the relationships between the distribution and abundance of species and abiotic or biotic factors	Sketch three scatter graphs to show the results when Spearman's rank correlation coefficient is 1, 0 and −1.			

CONTINUED

Now I can:	Show it	Needs more work	Almost there	Confident to move on
discuss the reasons for maintaining biodiversity and outline the ways in which biodiversity is conserved	For each of the three methods to conserve biodiversity, give one way of doing so.			
describe methods of assisted reproduction used in the conservation of endangered mammal species	State the two methods of assisted reproduction and compare them.			
explain why it is necessary to control invasive alien species	Give three ways that an alien species can affect an ecosystem.			
discuss the roles of the International Union for Conservation of Nature (IUCN) and the Convention on International Trade in Endangered Species of Wild Fauna and Flora (CITES) in global conservation	State the aims of IUCN and CITES.			
distinguish core information from other instructional text	Make a flashcard about how to extract core information from longer questions.			

19 Genetic technology

It is important that you are able to remember definitions of key terms for each topic. These will not only help your general understanding of a topic, but will also be necessary if you face a 'define' question in an exam.

Define	give the precise meaning

Look out for the two 'define' questions in this chapter, but also make sure that you are able to remember the definitions of all the key terms in the chapter.

19.1 Genetic engineering

1 What is genetic engineering?

2 Genetic engineering creates a transgenic organism by using a vector.

    a Explain one difference between the vectors used in genetic engineering and the vectors involved in the transmission of malaria. [2]

    b A transgenic organism carries recombinant DNA. Define 'recombinant DNA'. [1]

[Total: 3]

19.2 Tools for the gene technologist

1 What are the three ways to get the desired gene for genetic engineering?

2 What are two ways transgenic bacteria can be identified?

« RECALL AND CONNECT 1 «

Think back to Chapter 1 Cell structure: What is the difference between the circular DNA and plasmids in bacteria? Give two differences between eukaryotic DNA and prokaryotic DNA.

19.3 Gene editing

1 Define the term 'gene editing'.

2 The CRISPR/Cas9 system is a technique in which DNA can be inserted or removed at a precise point in the genome. The Cas9 nuclease protein cuts DNA using a RNA sequence called guide RNA (gRNA) at a sequence that is complementary to the gRNA. The break in the DNA can be repaired by adding one or more nucleotides, or by inserting a short double stand of DNA with aspeiric base pair sequence.

    a Suggest two ways that the CRISPR/Cas9 system can be used to edit genes and their effects. [4]

    b Describe the roles of Cas9 and gRNA in the CRISPR/Cas9 system. [2]

[Total: 6]

19.4 Separating and amplifying DNA

1 How can each of the following genetic techniques be used in forensics?

a polymerase chain reaction (PCR)

b gel electrophoresis

2 What is the name of the DNA polymerase used in PCR?

3 Four sisters have a family history of Huntington's disease. They wish to find out if they have inherited the faulty allele for this genetic condition. A small sample of their DNA is collected by a scientist for further analysis.

The scientist first conducts a PCR on the DNA sample.

a Explain why it is essential to conduct a PCR. [2]

b The PCR is done in three stages as listed. Briefly describe what occurs in each stage, including the conditions required for each stage.

   i Denaturation [3]

   ii Annealing [3]

   iii Extension [3]

[Total: 11]

> **UNDERSTAND THESE TERMS**
> - polymerase chain reaction (PCR)
> - gel electrophoresis

19.5 Analysing and storing genetic information

1 What are two uses of microarrays?

2 The *BRCA1* and *BRCA2* genes in human cells are responsible for repairing damaged DNA. However, mutations in these genes are found to be the cause of 5–10% of all breast cancer cases and about 60% of inherited breast cancer cases.

Explain how microarrays can be used in determining if an individual has a mutated form of the *BRCA* genes. [8]

[Total: 8]

> **UNDERSTAND THESE TERMS**
> - microarray/gene or DNA chips
> - DNA hybridisation
> - bioinformatics

19.6 Genetic technology and medicine

1 Copy the table and put a cross in the appropriate boxes to show how each genetic technique is used.

	Used as treatment for an adult or a born child	Used as treatment for a developing fetus	Used in diagnosis
Genetic engineering			
Genetic screening			

2   Give one benefit and one concern of genetic technology in medicine.

3   Different genetic technologies have been developed to support medical
    diagnosis and treatments.

    a   State how each genetic technique is used in medicine.
        i   Genetic engineering   [1]
        ii   Genetic screening   [1]
        iii   Gene therapy   [1]
    b   Describe two reasons why gene therapy is not always useful in treating
        genetic conditions.   [2]

                                                              [Total: 5]

19.7 Genetic technology and agriculture

1   What are some traits that are added to crop plants and animals to boost
    food production?

2   What is a biological and economical concern for GM plants and animals
    in agriculture?

3   Many maize plants have been genetically modified to gain specific traits
    to benefit farmers. A large proportion of maize plants currently growing
    in the USA are resistant to herbicides, insects and drought conditions.

    a   Explain why it is beneficial that maize plants are resistant to herbicides.   [3]

    b   Maize plants are often eaten by various pest insects such as root worms.
        These insects feed on the roots of maize plants. Nowadays, many maize
        plants are genetically modified to make the Bt toxin, which kills any pest
        insects that eat them. Bt toxins originate from *Bacillus thuringiensis*,
        a bacteria that is now commonly used as a biological pesticide.
        i   Suggest how root worms may affect the growth of maize plants.   [6]
        ii   Suggest how maize plants can be genetically modified to make
              the Bt toxin.   [5]
        iii   Explain how GM maize crops increase the profit made by farmers.   [2]

    c   Give two ecological concerns that people may have for genetically
        modifying crops for agriculture.   [2]

                                                              [Total: 18]

REFLECTION

How did you find this chapter? How can you find out what you know and don't know? Learning this much content can be overwhelming at times, so have a think about how you could help yourself learn and memorise key content and definitions while getting enough rest breaks.

SELF-ASSESSMENT CHECKLIST

Let's revisit the Knowledge focus and Exam skills focus for this chapter.

Decide how confident you are with each statement.

Now I can:	Show it	Needs more work	Almost there	Confident to move on
explain the principles of genetic technology	Draw a flowchart to show the general steps in genetic engineering.			
describe the tools and techniques available to the genetic engineer	Continue building on the flowchart you drew on genetic engineering by adding in details of the chemicals needed to conduct those steps.			
describe and explain the polymerase chain reaction (PCR) and gel electrophoresis	Draw a circular flowchart to show the steps in PCR and the conditions required in each step. Draw an annotated diagram of the setup for gel electrophoresis, including descriptions of how the DNA fragments are separated and seen.			
describe the uses of PCR and gel electrophoresis	Make a list of how PCR and gel electrophoresis are used.			
explain the use of microarrays	Draw an annotated diagram of a microarray to explain how they are interpreted and used in medicine.			

CONTINUED

Now I can:	Show it	Needs more work	Almost there	Confident to move on
outline the uses of databases that hold information about gene sequences, genomes and proteins	State three ways in which these databases are used.			
describe some examples of the uses of genetic technology in medicine	State four genetic techniques used in medical diagnosis and/or treatments and give at least one example in each.			
describe some uses of genetically modified organisms (GMOs) in agriculture	Give examples of GMOs in agriculture and explain the benefits of each modification.			
discuss the social and ethical implications of gene technology in medicine and food production	Draw a table to list the benefits and concerns of gene technology in medicine and agriculture.			
show that I understand the command word 'define' and can answer 'define' questions	Prepare definition flip cards for all key terms in the chapter and make sure you know the definition for each term.			

Exam practice 8

This section contains past paper questions from previous Cambridge exams, which draw together your knowledge on a range of topics that you have covered up to this point. These questions give you the opportunity to test your knowledge and understanding. Additional past paper practice questions can be found in the accompanying digital material.

The following question has an example student response and commentary provided. Work through the question first, then compare your answer to the sample response and commentary. Are your answers different to the sample responses?

1 a   Oil palm plantations in Malaysia and Indonesia have been created by cutting down rainforests. This reduces biodiversity.

Outline reasons why it is important to maintain biodiversity. [5]

   b   Palm oil companies are now being asked to produce palm oil in a sustainable way. This means that no more deforestation should take place.

Suggest ways in which individual consumers can encourage manufacturers to use palm oil from sustainable sources. [2]

[Total: 7]

Cambridge International AS & A Level Biology (9700) Paper 41, Q8b,c, November 2020

Example student response	Commentary
1 a Conservation is important because we may lose precious resources that future generations may use. Well maintained locations may also boost ecotourism and it is pleasing to enjoy (aesthetic reasons). A lack of biodiversity may also mean less food is available in the food chain.	The student has covered the major reasons for maintaining biodiversity – ecological, economical and aesthetic benefits. One more reason is needed for the last mark, where the student may elaborate on other ecological benefits, for example about the benefits of variation. *This answer is awarded 4 out of 5 marks.*
b Don't buy palm oil made from wood and forests.	The student needs to include the idea of not buying from unsustainable sources in addition to other ideas. For example, the student can mention how people can have better awareness for sustainability and donations to charities dedicated to conservation and anti-deforestation. *This answer is awarded 0 out of 2 marks.*

Now attempt an additional question. Use the previous sample response and commentary to guide you as you answer.

2   The aye-aye, *Daubentonia madagascariensis*, is a primate native to Madagascar. Aye-ayes are nocturnal (active at night) and make their nests high up in trees. They feed on insect larvae in the trunks of trees.

Fig. 8.1 shows an aye-aye.

Fig. 8.1

The International Union for Conservation of Nature (IUCN) is the world's largest global environmental organisation. The IUCN Red List of Threatened Species™ evaluates the conservation status of plant and animal species.

The aye-aye is categorised as endangered on the IUCN Red List, which means that it faces a very high risk of becoming extinct in the wild.

a   Name the domain to which the aye-aye belongs.   [1]

b   Suggest one reason why aye-ayes have become endangered.   [1]

c   Suggest ways in which zoos may help to protect this species
    from extinction.   [3]

[Total: 5]

Cambridge International AS & A Level Biology (9700) Paper 42, Q1a, March 2018

The next question has an example student response and commentary provided. Work through the question first, then compare your answer to the sample response and commentary. Are your answers different to the sample responses? What information does this give you about your understanding of the topic?

3   Severe combined immunodeficiency (SCID) is a group of life-threatening diseases. SCID is caused by mutations that prevent the normal function of the immune system. Infants born with SCID are at very high risk of infectious diseases.

One feature of SCID is that T-lymphocytes do not develop normally.

In the development of normal T-lymphocytes, the production of circular pieces of DNA called T-lymphocyte receptor excision circles (TRECs) is an important event.

It is possible to use the polymerase chain reaction (PCR) to detect TRECs in DNA extracted from a sample of blood. The results of this reaction can be used to identify children with SCID.

a i Describe the role of the primers in the PCR used for the detection of TRECs. [3]

 ii Suggest **and** explain how the results of PCR for the detection of TRECs can be used to identify children with SCID. [2]

b One form of SCID is caused by a mutation that results in a deficiency of the enzyme adenosine deaminase (ADA).

Children with ADA-deficient SCID can be treated with gene therapy using a virus. After successful gene therapy, the children are able to produce ADA for themselves.

Suggest how children with ADA-deficient SCID can be treated with gene therapy using a virus. [3]

[Total: 8]

Cambridge International AS & A Level Biology (9700) Paper 42, Q2a,c, March 2020

Example student response	Commentary
3 a i Primers bind to the TRECs to signal the section to amplify. The DNA polymerase can recognise the primer and start building the new strand. This ensures only the TREC DNA is replicated.	The 2 marks are awarded for describing DNA polymerase as being able to bind to where the primer is and reference to its specificity. The first statement about how primers bind needs more details, for example explain how the primer is able to bind to the DNA. *This answer is awarded 2 out of 3 marks.*
ii If a child has high levels of TREC in the PCR result then they have SCID. The TREC DNA can be bound with a dye to make it visible.	Although the student has the correct idea on how to use PCR results, they did not read the question carefully, where it says TREC is present if T-lymphocytes are developing normally. Therefore, a child with high TREC levels does not have SCID. It will be the opposite. *This answer is awarded 0 out of 2 marks.*
b Extract the gene that codes for ADA from a healthy person. Take a cell from the child and insert the genes into the DNA in it. Insert the cell with the recombinant DNA back into the child's bone marrow.	The student has a clear understanding of how gene therapy is done, which is inserting a healthy allele into the child's own cells. One thing to improve is to specify what kind of cell is taken from the child, since it should be referring to cells in the bone marrow and/or T cells. *This answer is awarded 2 out of 3 marks.*

Now attempt two additional questions on a similar topic. Use the previous sample response and commentary to guide you as you answer.

4   Calcitonin is a small protein hormone consisting of 32 amino acids. One of its functions is to inhibit the activity of cells, called osteoclasts, that break down bone tissue.

Calcitonin has been used as a therapeutic protein to treat osteoporosis. In osteoporosis too much breakdown of bone tissue in older people leads to reduced bone density and a risk of breaking bones.

a   Compared to human calcitonin, salmon calcitonin is more biologically active. It remains active in the human body for longer and binds to calcitonin receptors more readily.

Bioinformatics was used to identify this more biologically active form of calcitonin to treat osteoporosis.

Explain how bioinformatics helped identify salmon calcitonin as a suitable form of calcitonin to treat human osteoporosis.   [2]

b   Salmon calcitonin to treat osteoporosis is made by genetically engineered *Escherichia coli* bacteria. To produce these bacteria, a plasmid was cut and joined to the new gene to form a recombinant plasmid. The recombinant plasmid was then introduced into the bacterial cells.

i   Name an enzyme that can:

• cut plasmid DNA

• join the salmon calcitonin gene with plasmid DNA.   [2]

ii   Identify **and** explain two properties of plasmids that allow them to be used as vectors in gene cloning.   [2]

[Total: 6]

Cambridge International AS & A Level Biology (9700) Paper 42, Q3bii,c, November 2019

Have a go at another past paper question.

5   The β-globin gene codes for the β-globin polypeptide of haemoglobin. It has two alleles, **Hb^A** (normal) and **Hb^S** (sickle cell). The sickle cell allele differs from the normal allele due to a base substitution mutation and this mutation results in a single amino acid change to the β-globin polypeptide.

There are three possible genotypes and phenotypes.

• **Hb^S Hb^S**, sickle cell anaemia, a severe disease

• **Hb^A Hb^S**, sickle cell trait with mild or no symptoms of sickle cell anaemia

• **Hb^A Hb^A**, normal (healthy)

A man and woman who both have sickle cell trait may choose to have children by IVF. This allows the genotype of embryos to be determined by gene testing before the embryos are implanted. Embryos with the normal genotype can then be selected and implanted into the mother.

One technique that can be used in gene testing an embryo for the **Hb**^{S} allele is restriction fragment length polymorphism (RFLP) analysis. This involves digesting a DNA sample from an embryo with a restriction endonuclease and then separating the DNA fragments by gel electrophoresis. The position of the DNA fragments on the gel can show if the embryo has the **Hb**^{S} allele.

a The first step in testing an embryo for the **Hb**^{S} allele by RFLP analysis requires many copies of the part of the β-globin gene in which the mutation causing sickle cell anaemia occurs.

   i Name the technique used to produce many copies of a DNA sequence from a small quantity of DNA. [1]

   ii Explain why it is necessary to copy this DNA sequence many times in order to test embryos for **Hb**^{S} alleles by RFLP analysis. [1]

In the next step of RFLP analysis, the copies of the part of the β-globin gene from the first step are incubated with a restriction endonuclease, *Mst*II. This enzyme cuts at a specific sequence of DNA (the restriction site).

The restriction site for *Mst*II is shown in Fig. 5.1.

5′ – C C T N A G G – 3′
3′ – G G A N T C C – 5′   N = any nucleotide (A, T, C or G)

Fig. 5.1

Fig. 5.2 shows the part of an **Hb**^{A} allele obtained from the first step. All the *Mst*II restriction sites and the number of DNA base pairs separating these restriction sites are shown.

Hb^A

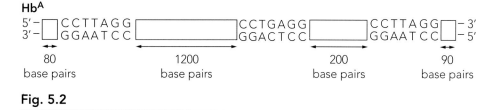

Fig. 5.2

Fig. 5.3 shows the same part of an **Hb**^{S} allele. The single base substitution in the **Hb**^{S} allele that causes sickle cell anaemia is indicated.

Hb^S

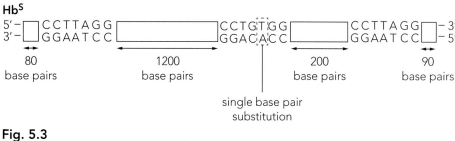

Fig. 5.3

b   With reference to Fig. 5.1, Fig. 5.2 and Fig. 5.3, explain why the enzyme
    *Mst*II can be used in RFLP analysis to show the difference between these
    parts of the **Hb^A** and **Hb^S** alleles.   [4]

c   After cutting with *Mst*II, the DNA fragments are separated by gel
    electrophoresis. Explain how gel electrophoresis separates DNA
    fragments cut with restriction endonucleases.   [3]

d   Four embryos, **1, 2, 3** and **4**, were tested for the **Hb^S** allele using RFLP
    analysis. Fig. 5.4 shows the DNA fragments separated by gel electrophoresis
    for the four embryos. The DNA fragments for two individuals of known
    genotype, homozygous for **Hb^A** and homozygous for **Hb^S**, are also shown.

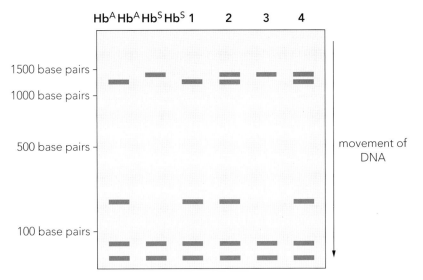

Fig. 5.4

i   State the purpose of using DNA from individuals homozygous
    for **Hb^A** and **Hb^S**.   [1]

ii With reference to Fig. 5.4, complete Table 5.1 to show the
    genotypes of embryos **2, 3** and **4**.   [2]

embryo	genotype
1	Hb^A Hb^A
2	
3	
4	

Table 5.1

e   Discuss the ethical and social considerations of gene testing
    embryos for genetic diseases.   [3]

                                                                        [Total: 15]

Cambridge International AS & A Level Biology (9700) Paper 42, Q3, March 2018

The following question has an example student response and commentary provided. Work through the question first, then compare your answer to the sample response and commentary. Are your answers different to the sample responses? Do you feel you need to improve your understanding of this topic?

6 One method of testing a person's reaction time is to use an online, computer click timer test.

Some students carried out a test using the method described.

- Each student looks at a computer screen and clicks a start button on the screen and waits for the background colour to change.

- As soon as the background colour changes the student clicks a stop button on the screen.

- The reaction time appears on the screen.

A student in the class thought that boys had a faster reaction time than girls.

A group of students from the class decided to repeat the test to investigate the hypothesis: ***Boys have a faster reaction time than girls.***

a Identify the independent variable and the dependent variable in this investigation. [2]

b State the type of qualitative variable which best describes the independent variable. [1]

c Describe a method the students could use to collect the data needed to test their hypothesis.

Your method should be set out in a logical order and be detailed enough for another person to follow. [6]

d Suggest **one** feature of the online test which may be a source of error. [1]

[Total: 10]

Cambridge International AS & A Level Biology (9700) Paper 53, Q1a, June 2019

Example student response	Commentary
6 a Independent variable: Reaction time Dependent variable: Room condition	The student has the variables confused. Remember we change the independent variable, we measure the dependent variable and control variables are those we keep the same. *This answer is awarded 0 out of 2 marks.*
b Continuous since it is numerical.	Although this answer is not the same as the one in the mark scheme, the student has correctly named the type of variable based on their independent variable from **a**. *This answer is awarded 1 out of 1 mark.*

Example student response	Commentary
c Have 3 boys and 3 girls do this test. They should complete the test on a school computer in the same room. The room conditions should be kept constant throughout the experiment. They should repeat the test a few times to ensure there are no anomalies.	While the student made an attempt to standardise the test conditions and number of people in each gender group, there is insufficient detail on control variables, for example conditions of the room and participants. There was also no mention of how to ensure validity and reliability of the results. There should also be a reference to potential risks or evidence of considering this. *This answer is awarded 3 out of 6 marks.*
d Online lag	Any reference to how the online test itself would not work properly would be awarded a mark. Any answer relating to other aspects of the test will not get a mark. *This answer is awarded 1 out of 1 mark.*

7 Now that you've read through the commentary, attempt writing a mark scheme for question **6**. This will check that you've understood exactly why each mark has (or has not) been allocated. The more often you do this, and the better you get to know the way mark schemes are written, the more confident you will feel about your answers.

Practical skills for A Level

In this chapter you will answer questions on:

- practical skills
- planning an investigation
- constructing a hypothesis
- identifying variables
- describing the sequence of steps
- risk assessment
- recording and displaying results
- analysis, conclusions and evaluation
- evaluating evidence
- conclusions and discussion.

In this chapter you will:

- practise managing distribution of your time across the whole paper.

Students often spend too long on difficult questions, even if they are not worth many marks, so they don't have enough time to tackle other questions. It is crucial that you learn to manage your time well to ensure you can give a good answer to each question. As you work through the questions in this chapter, pay attention to the number of marks on offer and make sure you don't spend too long on questions with fewer marks. Try timing yourself as you answer questions; it is usually good if you can spend about one minute per mark.

P2.1 Practical skills

1   Decide if the following statements about practical skills are true or false.

   a   Repeating experiments and calculating a mean average gives more accurate results.

   b   Units should not be included in the body of a results table.

   c   All values in a row of a results table should be recorded to the same number of decimal places.

   d   In a line graph, the independent variable goes on the *x*-axis and the dependent variable goes on the *y*-axis. It is the opposite in a bar chart.

P2.2 Planning an investigation

1   Make a list of key points to include in a good experiment plan.

> ## « RECALL AND CONNECT 1 «
>
> Think back to Chapter P1 Practical skills for AS Level: What are the three types of variables and what does each mean?

P2.3 Constructing a hypothesis

1   What is the difference between a prediction and a hypothesis?

2   A student investigates how substrate concentration affects the rate of enzyme action.

   State the hypothesis for this experiment and explain your hypothesis using your own knowledge.   **[Total: 3]**

> ### UNDERSTAND THESE TERMS
> * prediction
> * hypothesis

P2.4 Identifying variables

1   In an experiment to investigate how the rate of amylase action is affected by the temperature, which of the following should be the key variables to standardise?

   A   Temperature
   B   Concentration of substrate
   C   Concentration of enzyme
   D   Concentration of products
   E   Light intensity

   F   Volume and concentration of iodine solution
   G   Time taken in the water bath
   H   Time taken for the reaction to run

2 What is the difference between a control experiment and a key variable to standardise?

3 A student is asked to investigate how light intensity affects the rate of photosynthesis.

    a Write a hypothesis for this investigation. [1]

    b Suggest how results may be collected in this experiment and explain your suggestion. [3]

    c One of the key variables to standardise in this experiment is the concentration of carbon dioxide.

        i Suggest two other key variables to standardise for this experiment. [2]

        ii The concentration of carbon dioxide can be standardised using a sodium bicarbonate ($NaHCO_3$) solution. Sodium bicarbonate has a relative molecular mass of 84.

           Describe how the student can make a $2\,mol\,dm^{-3}$ $NaHCO_3$ solution. [4]

        [Total: 10]

> **UNDERSTAND THESE TERMS**
> - continuous data
> - discrete data
> - ordinal data
> - nominal data
> - control experiment

P2.5 Describing the sequence of steps

1 How can each of the following be improved when writing an experiment plan?

    a Writing in full paragraphs

    b Write the plan out directly

    c Describe complicated setups

    d Give separate lists of steps and equipment

2 A student wants to investigate how different light colours affect the rate of photosynthesis in pondweed. They are provided with the following:

- a lamp
- pondweed
- three translucent light filters – red, blue and green
- beakers
- measuring cylinder
- a filter funnel
- 5% sodium bicarbonate solution
- metre ruler
- timer.

Write a plan to describe how the student can complete this investigation. **[Total: 7]**

P2.6 Risk assessment

1 What is a risk?

2 For each of the following scenarios, state one risk and suggest one way to minimise the risk.

   a Investigating the effects of temperature (10 °C to 80 °C) on enzyme action. [2]

   b Preparing a stained onion epidermal slide. [2]

   [Total: 4]

P2.7 Recording and displaying results

1 What is wrong with each statement?

   a There should not be units in any part of a results table.

   b The dependent variable goes on the *x*-axis of a graph.

   c Continuous data can be plotted by a bar chart.

2 A student did an experiment to investigate the rate of water uptake by plants under different light intensities. Their results table is shown.

Distance between lamp and plant	Volume of water taken up in 5 minutes / cm³			
	Trial 1	Trial 2	Trial 3	Mean
10 cm	23	25	21	23
30 cm	14	20	15	16.3
50 cm	8	7	2	5.7

Describe three ways that the student can improve their results table. **[Total: 3]**

P2.8 Analysis, conclusions and evaluation

1 What is the difference between a hypothesis and a null hypothesis?

2 What is the mean, median and mode value for this set of data?

   3 3 4 5 5 6 9 11 12 12 12

UNDERSTAND THESE TERMS

- mode (modal class)
- median
- standard deviation
- standard error (SE)
- null hypothesis

3 Copy and complete the table to decide what calculation each description is referring to.

Description	Calculation
Shows how spread out a data set is from its mean value	
Shows how close the mean value is likely to be to the true mean value	
To find if two data sets share a linear correlation	
To test if there is significant difference between two data sets	
To see if there is significant correlation between two data sets	
To find if there is significant difference between the observed data set to the expected data	

[Total: 6]

4 A restaurant owner wants to investigate whether antiseptic **A** or antiseptic **B** is best for killing bacteria. A scientist helped them set up five Petri dishes for each antiseptic, and grow the bacteria with either antiseptic. The number of bacterial colonies was counted in each case and recorded in the table.

Number of bacterial colonies	Antiseptic A	Antiseptic B
1	30	25
2	36	29
3	28	30
4	29	23
5	33	22
Standard deviation	3.27	3.56

a State the null hypothesis for this investigation. [1]

b Using the equation provided, calculate the t-value between antiseptics **A** and **B**. [3]

$$t = \frac{(x_1 - x_2)}{\sqrt{\frac{s_1^2}{n_1} + \frac{s_2^2}{n_2}}}$$

c   Using the critical value table below, and the calculated value from **b**, determine whether one antiseptic is better than the other in killing bacteria.   [3]

Degrees of freedom	Value of t			
1	6.31	12.7	63.7	63.6
2	2.92	4.30	9.93	31.6
3	2.35	3.18	5.84	12.9
4	2.13	2.78	4.60	8.61
5	2.02	2.57	4.03	6.87
6	1.94	2.45	3.71	5.96
7	1.90	2.37	3.50	5.41
8	1.86	2.31	3.36	5.04
9	1.83	2.26	3.25	4.78
10	1.81	2.23	3.17	4.59
11	1.80	2.20	3.11	4.44
12	1.78	2.18	3.06	4.32
13	1.77	2.16	3.01	4.22
14	1.76	2.15	2.98	4.14
15	1.75	2.13	2.95	4.07
16	1.75	2.12	2.92	4.02
17	1.74	2.11	2.90	3.97
18	1.73	2.10	2.88	3.92
19	1.73	2.09	2.86	3.88
20	1.73	2.09	2.85	3.85
22	1.72	2.07	2.82	3.79
24	1.71	2.06	2.80	3.75
26	1.71	2.06	2.78	3.71
28	1.70	2.05	2.76	3.67
30	1.70	2.04	2.75	3.65
>30	1.64	1.96	2.58	3.29
Probability that chance could have produced this value of t	0.10	0.05	0.01	0.001
Confidence level	10%	5%	1%	0.1%

d   Explain how significant difference can be determined graphically.   [3]

[Total: 10]

P2.9 Evaluating evidence

1   When evaluating the reliability and validity of the results, what are some key
    points to consider?

P2.10 Conclusions and discussion

1   What should be included in the conclusion of an experiment?

2   A student investigated the effect of light intensity on the rate of photosynthesis
    using the setup shown in Figure P2.1. The student collected the results and plotted
    a graph, shown in Figure P2.2.

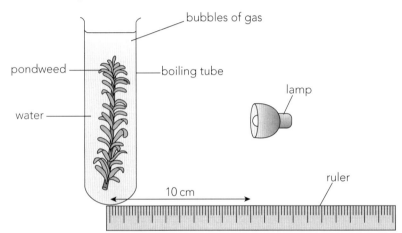

Figure P2.1

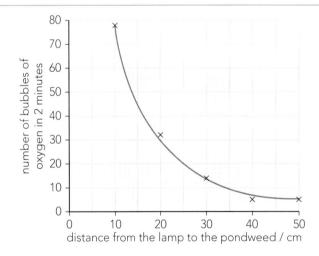

Figure P2.2

a   Describe and explain the results shown in Figure P2.2.   [3]

b   Using Figure P2.1, suggest two ways that the experiment may be
    improved.   [4]

[Total: 7]

≪ RECALL AND CONNECT 2 ≪

Think back to Chapter 13 Photosynthesis: What is the purpose of water in the photosynthesis reaction? Where does photophosphorylation occur? What is the name of the enzyme that catalyses the reaction between carbon dioxide and ribulose bisphosphate? Apart from RuBP, what are the other two key substrates in the Calvin cycle?

REFLECTION

How did you find this chapter about practical skills? Were you able to manage your time effectively across all of the questions? For any parts that you are not so confident in, what can you do to improve them? Many students find experiment planning and interpreting graphs rather tricky – what can you do to make this process easier? Consider what the key aspects of these two types of questions are and how you can be familiar with them.

SELF-ASSESSMENT CHECKLIST

Let's revisit the Knowledge focus and Exam skills focus for this chapter.

Decide how confident you are with each statement.

Now I can:	Show it	Needs more work	Almost there	Confident to move on
define a problem in a given context, including stating a prediction and constructing a hypothesis	Find an experiment that you have done or will do, and write a hypothesis, explaining your prediction.			
plan an investigation to test a hypothesis or to investigate a problem, identifying the independent variable and the dependent variable, and listing key variables to standardise	Following the same experiment, write the independent variable and the dependent variable. List two control variables and describe how to keep them the same.			
describe how the independent variable would be altered, how the dependent variable would be measured, and how the key variables would be standardised	Following the same experiment, describe how the independent variable will be changed and how the dependent variable would be measured.			

CONTINUED

Now I can:	Show it	Needs more work	Almost there	Confident to move on
describe how any control experiments would be used	Following the same experiment, design a control setup and explain why it should be used.			
describe a logical sequence of steps for the investigation, including identification of any risks and how they can be minimised	Following the same experiment, write down the steps you would take to complete the investigation. State two potential risks (if any) and explain how they can be minimised.			
describe how to make up solutions in per cent (mass per volume) and in $mol\,dm^{-3}$	Write the steps taken to make a 1% solution and a $1\,mol\,dm^{-3}$ solution with glucose. The relative molecular mass for glucose is 180.			
assess validity of results by identifying anomalous results, looking at the spread of results and using standard deviation, standard error or 95% confidence intervals (CI)	Write out the equation for standard deviation and explain what each symbol means. Write one sentence to describe what standard deviation shows and how it can be plotted on a graph.			
calculate standard error, and use it to draw error bars on graphs and to interpret apparent differences between two sets of data	Write out the equation for standard error and explain what each symbol means. Write one sentence to describe what standard error shows and how it can be plotted on a graph.			
state a null hypothesis for a statistical test	Explain the difference between a null hypothesis and a hypothesis.			
use a t-test to find the probability that differences between two sets of data are due to chance	Write out the equation for t-test and explain what each symbol means. Write one sentence to describe what t-test shows and how its significance can be determined.			

CONTINUED

Now I can:	Show it	Needs more work	Almost there	Confident to move on
use Pearson's linear correlation to find out if two sets of data have a linear relationship	Sketch a graph with two trend lines, showing two pairs of data that have Pearson's value of −1 and +1.			
use Spearman's rank correlation to find out if two sets of data are correlated	Describe the difference between Spearman's rank correlation and Pearson's linear correlation.			
justify the choice of statistical test used	Make a list of all statistical tests covered in the syllabus and write one sentence for each, summarising the aim of each test.			
manage distribution of my time across the whole paper	Time yourself when doing practice questions and see how long you take. Alternatively, set yourself a stop clock when doing each exam skills question, aiming to have 1 minute per mark.			

> Acknowledgements

The authors and publishers acknowledge the following sources of copyright material and are grateful for the permissions granted. While every effort has been made, it has not always been possible to identify the sources of all the material used, or to trace all copyright holders. If any omissions are brought to our notice, we will be happy to include the appropriate acknowledgements on reprinting.

Cambridge International copyright material in this publication is reproduced under licence and remains the intellectual property of Cambridge Assessment International Education. Cambridge Assessment International Education bears no responsibility for the example answers to questions taken from its past question papers which are contained in this publication.

Thanks to the following for permission to reproduce images:

Cover Coldimages/Getty Images; *Inside* **Unit 1** Clouds Hill Imaging Ltd/Getty Images; Callista Images/Getty Images; Biophoto Associates/Science Photo Library; **Unit 5** Biophoto Associates; Eric Grave/Science Photo Library; David M. Phillips/Science Photo Library; Michael Abbey/ Science Photo Library; **Unit 7** Visuals Unlimited/Science Photo Library; Don W. Fawcett/ Science Photo Library; Science Photo Library; David M. Phillips/Science Photo Library; **Unit 12** Don W. Fawcett/Science Photo Library; **Unit 13** Biology Pics/Science Photo Library; Biophoto Associates/Science Photo Library; Watcha/Getty Images; **Unit 17** Paul D Stewart/ Science Photo Library; **Unit 18** Laura Hedien/Getty Images; James Stone/Getty Images; Thorsten Negro/Getty Images.